Altar(ed) Girl

*One Woman's True Story of
Confronting Clergy Sexual Abuse*

C.M. Morgan

BALBOA.
PRESS
A DIVISION OF HAY HOUSE

Balboa Press books may be ordered through booksellers or by contacting:

Balboa Press
A Division of Hay House
1663 Liberty Drive
Bloomington, IN 47403
www.balboapress.com
1 (877) 407-4847

Because of the dynamic nature of the Internet, any web addresses or
links contained in this book may have changed since publication and
may no longer be valid. The views expressed in this work are solely those
of the author and do not necessarily reflect the views of the publisher,
and the publisher hereby disclaims any responsibility for them.

The author of this book does not dispense medical advice or prescribe the use
of any technique as a form of treatment for physical, emotional, or medical
problems without the advice of a physician, either directly or indirectly. The
intent of the author is only to offer information of a general nature to help
you in your quest for emotional and spiritual well-being. In the event you use
any of the information in this book for yourself, which is your constitutional
right, the author and the publisher assume no responsibility for your actions.

Any people depicted in stock imagery provided by Thinkstock are
models, and such images are being used for illustrative purposes only.
Certain stock imagery © Thinkstock.

Printed in the United States of America.

ISBN: 978-1-4525-8891-9 (sc)
ISBN: 978-1-4525-8892-6 (e)

Library of Congress Control Number: 2013923107

Balboa Press rev. date: 1/14/2014

I dreamed of being an altar boy…
not an altered girl.

Contents

Chapter One... 1

Chapter Two... 5

Chapter Three 11

Chapter Four 19

Chapter Five... 24

Chapter Six... 32

Chapter Seven 38

Chapter Eight.. 48

Chapter Nine.. 56

Chapter Ten.. 61

Chapter Eleven.. 69

Chapter Twelve.. 77

Epilogue 85

Chapter One

Spring 2010 — Los Angeles, CA

I'm in Running Springs, California for two weeks to help my Pops recover from hip replacement surgery. This is the same guy with whom I stopped talking in my late 20's. Now I'm making his lunch, helping him down the steps with his walker and driving him to doctor appointments. I live in St. Cloud, MN and for the past year I Skype with my dad most every Sunday evening. I have my lovely partner Ashlynn to thank for the consistency of these weekly phone calls. I really did not think my dad cared one way or the other, he wears his logic on his sleeve and his emotions are tucked away in a drawer somewhere in downtown businessville. But after the first few video-chats, Ashlynn noticed that he really likes talking with me, that it's good for me to have this relationship with my dad. I believe her and so, now I'm back here in California assisting with his recovery.

On any given Sunday afternoon, she would ask, "Hey, you gonna Skype with your dad tonight?" The first few times she did this, I could not understand why she was asking, I was suspicious… of what, I don't know. Why did she care if I talked to my dad? She told me that my dad looks forward to these chats. I was honestly puzzled, having never had a solid, enjoyable relationship with my father since my teen years, and I never had a partner who truly cared about my relationships with my biological family. Then one day, it happened – I got a text message from my Pops! My 78-year old dad was texting me from his little flip phone mobile, "Hey u pops here Skype later?" With the biggest smile on my face, I about cried.

He lives in the mountains with my wonderful step-mom Marilyn, works full time in private practice as a clinical psychologist and had been trying to manage the painful degeneration of his right hip joint for about eight months. A doctor finally managed to see that it needed to be replaced and so he got the surgery last week. My Pops - who never needs any type of pain medication, hasn't imbibed in alcohol or smoked anything in over 25 years, ran more marathons than I know about and still rides his Harley Deuce, now in trike form - had to get surgery. It is his first serious surgery and so I cancelled work for a couple of weeks to help him out. It was an odd choice for me to make on so many levels and of course, Ashlynn was completely supportive.

She keeps suggesting that I write, so I finally attempt the feat. She suggests that I write "my story" and my inner cynic replies quickly, "Everyone has their own story, who cares about mine?" Then, when I slow down and sit quiet, I become aware, once again, that it's just my ego blabbering on. I've learned that ego likes to swing in an algebraic sort of way with its "I'm greater than/less than (but not equal to) you" formula. Stating that my story is not important, which I know is a false, self-defeating thought, keeps me in a moment of focused attention from others who will then say, "No, really C.M., you should write…" And so it goes, avoiding attentive care to my soul for fear of becoming too self-focused keeps the focus on my fear. So I just let go and let love take the reins.

I am not even sure how to write this story. Do I continue in a chronological manner or just do the stream of consciousness, rapid writing method. My brain wants to control the process: *Attention! All thoughts will now proceed in a calm and orderly manner!* I keep a watchful third-eye on any memories or ideas that might stray out of line, then watch them run wild through my hands as I type and I learn that it truly is good to write your story.

In the quiet moments, when I sit long enough to feel my own heart beating, I go deep inside and find the true self. Stepping up and to the right of my ego lives all that beautiful spirit/core/ fire/unearthly unself of pure light energy and love. Thesaurus describes the antonym of ego as humility, meekness and servility. Humble, yes. Meek and servile? No and sometimes. I'm often just one of the masses holding the massiveness of all one-pure-love. I'm okay with the idea that my presence is just one in the crowd. When I'm stuck in traffic on the freeway, I acquiesce to the knowledge that I am part of that traffic slowing me down. I am part of that long line causing me to wait in a long line and I find it somehow comforting, a reminder that I am one of us. We're all one of the same universal light just walking around in different bodies. The human part is just a soul delivery system… or maybe it's the other way around, I can't remember.

Sugar, the pint-sized Chihuahua scratches at my chest and even though she's already sitting cozy in the crook of my arm she wants more, wants to go deeper in order to get more comfortable. I mean, don't we all want that, just in reverse? I prefer to get more comfortable before I go deeper and for the past few years, I kept trying to snuggle my way toward stability so the depth would be easier to digest, so I could breathe without a regulator, so I could think and not feel but it just didn't happen that way, not for me, anyway. So I try to listen to my guides instead of my ego.

My guides communicate to me in ways they know I'll recognize. They're smart like that. They apparently know that I like numbers lined up in time or space. Like when I wake up gently from a sound sleep and the clock shows 3:33 or 4:44. Or when I look at the clock for no reason during the day and it reads 12:34. My favorite is 11:11 - AM or PM doesn't matter, I see it when I need a nudge. Like when I randomly glance at my odometer for the first time in months and it shows 77,777 miles. These things always get a smile of gratitude and if you find me saying, "Thanks" to no-one in particular, look around… there's probably a clock nearby.

They send me animals, too, and like Sugar, I'm scratching to go deeper here with this story because it's no longer comfortable walking around on the surface. I shift again, a new gear for me and I no longer ask for guidance because it's always already there. I now ask for help to see the guidance, to follow it without forethought or doubt. It reminds me of the trust walks we used to take during the Catholic school catechism class when I was a pre-teenager. We would pair up and hold hands; one of us blindfolded while the other guided us around the church grounds or the beach-camp during a weekend retreat. The lesson, of course, was to learn to trust your partner but in retrospect, I wish they directed us to focus on trusting ourselves while being guided by someone or something that could see more clearly, the path that lie ahead. THAT would have been the lesson to last a lifetime.

Chapter Two

When others want to tell me about something that happened to them or an event that occurred and they say, "Well, I don't know where to start" I usually reply, "Just start in the middle and work your way out." So I'll take my own advice and start in the middle of my story.

The year was 1988, I was 28 years old and the universe had conspired to support me, as usual. Apparently, it was time for me to confront Benjamin Stringer, aka Father Ben Stringer, one of the men who sexually abused me when I was a child. I was completely unaware of what was about to unfold and of how this jigsaw of a journey would fall into place.

My good pal Maggie and I were living together in Mill Valley, California which is located in Marin County about 15 miles from the northern end of the Golden Gate Bridge. We had a great time together riding our motorcycles throughout Marin, as much as time would allow. We rode up around Mt. Tamalpias overlooking the Pacific, went North to wine country, over the bridge to join Dykes on Bikes in the Pride parades, to the beaches and beyond.

We were still in our 20's, laughed most of the time, and danced in the living room to the Fine Young Cannibals, Little Feat and Erasure blasting from the turntable. We finished each other's sentences. She was my first best friend.

Maggie was employed by a forestry consulting firm and planned to spend that summer working a project on Bainbridge Island up near Seattle, Washington. We had been intimate with each other, the proverbial 'friends with benefits' type of relationship and so, not wanting to spend the whole summer apart, we agreed that I would visit for a long weekend. It was an easy decision, a little vacation to a new place that neither of us had seen before. Although we had built a solid bond that summer, our relationship has ebbed and flowed throughout the years simply because we've both moved around so much, losing contact here and there. However, I called her last week and it was like we never left the living room... more on that later.

I was working as an auto mechanic at a women-owned shop in San Rafael. Our crew of three women and two men wrenched on German and Japanese cars, but Volkswagen's were our mainstay. It was a pretty great scene for a while. After work, Deidre, the owner, let us stay at the shop and tinker with our own vehicles. I learned how to rebuild the engine and the clutch on my '78 VW Bus. I replaced the brakes, air and fuel lines and also learned about torque. For the mechanically challenged, torque is simply a measure of pressure or tightness using foot-pounds. Some screws and bolts require a specific amount of pressure on the torque. For example, the 10 mm nuts on the oil sump plate for a VW bug require a torque of five foot-pounds each. Any tighter and you'll strip the stud requiring the mechanic to split the engine case and replace the stud. That's way more hours than anyone wants to spend on a simple oil change. Wrenching taught me much about fixing what's broken; I learned that you have to strip a few screws before you learn the torque.

Starting in my late teens, I went to see many different therapists. My mother took me to my first therapist once she learned that I was a member of the "Lesbian Nation." She actually found me sleeping with a friend when I was 18 years old. I was still living with mom and I truly was just sleeping, but because we were both on my single-sized mattress and the other one was empty, Mom figured it out. Her daughter was a Dyke and she had to fix that quick.

The psychiatrist was an odd, creepy sort of character and his office smelled like old food. I was his last client on a Friday and he seemed completely bored with his job. The building was an older, converted army-corps type office building, hollow and empty, not unlike the therapist himself. Neither of us had anything to offer the other, so the search for the cure ended after the second session. That was mom's first and final attempt to rid me of the gay.

It was not until my mid 20's that I sought out therapy of my own accord. I found many wonderful older crones to assist me on this path but I never stayed long enough to thoroughly work through anything. In retrospect, I think it was perfect how it all played out. Each one taught me something, showed me new perspectives as old issues spiraled back around in new situations. These teachers, all womyn, have appeared consistently and easily throughout my life, not only in the therapist office, but also in numerous other places I chose to appear: the softball field, the Womyn's Music Festivals, the Brick Hut Café, the twelve-step meetings. I have always been so grateful to these teachers who taught me the concepts of deep love, process, communication and spirituality.

It was sometime after Maggie and I made our Seattle plans that I began to think about looking for Stringer. It was strange, how it came to me. I mean, I didn't plan to think about it or to even start that journey. It just happened without me realizing it. I had shared a lot with Maggie about my childhood, she knew about the sexual abuse from Stringer, another priest named Brogan; a childhood neighbor named Harvey Shirley, those guys in high school and the physical, mental and emotional abuse from my parents. One day I just found myself telling Maggie that I wanted to confront Stringer, to get an apology or something. I wasn't really sure what I wanted, but because he was the only other person in the rooms with me when I was so young, I knew I needed some type of validation. A tiny part of me had always felt that maybe that I had made up the whole sick story. I hate that aspect of abuse where self-doubt leads to self-suspicion.

I was attending the Thursday night Sister's in Sobriety AA meetings during that time, and began to talk more about my thoughts on confronting *this* perpetrator. Note: I had originally spoken of *my* perpetrator, but writing it now seems so weirdly privileged in a twisted way. It is important to understand that being sexually violated by a priest, a veritable 'man of God', brings layers upon layers of confusing thoughts and feelings, none of which are pleasant and loving, such as: I'm special enough to be 'chosen' by this priest, but I'm filthy enough to be taken by Satan if I tell anyone. Understanding my own worth was impossible. I have since learned that he was, in fact, not relegated to perpetrating only me, but he had violated others as well.

The women at the meetings gifted me with much support and compassion. Some shared their experience, strength and hope while others shared their fears, concerns and disappointments at missed opportunities to do the same. It was the first time I had openly discussed this clergy abuse and it felt good to do so. It felt like a coming out, of sorts, and it seemed to give other women the green light to share their secrets as well. Still, at that time, I did not know anyone else who shared this type of abuse. It was a lonely issue.

Orchestrated on another plane and unbeknownst to me, specific people were showing up in my life for very specific reasons and as it happens, I had befriended a woman named Lindsey. She had brought her car into the shop for a fix and being Deidre's friend, she sometimes stayed around and chatted for a bit. Lindsey was also a Sheriff in Marin County. She had plenty of experience working with pedophiles in the prisons and so we began to talk about what I would do if I ever saw Stringer again... the perpetrator, the criminal, the thief who robbed me of so much innocence and self-love. It was a very scary thing to even think about let alone actually talk about.

Lindsey and I discussed all the possibilities that could happen *if* I confronted Stringer. He could deny everything, he could admit some things or he could call the police and charge me for harassment. Lindsey told me that if I find him at his house, I should put my foot in the doorway to prevent him from shutting the door. I tried to picture what this would look like and from what I remember as a young girl, he was a pretty big guy - stronger than me of course. He had dark, slicked back hair and thick black-framed glasses. His face was ruddy and red, and his look was that of an experienced alcoholic. What is interesting is that, every time I thought about the confrontation, I thought about it in terms of me being eight years old. Even though I was an adult womon, my little self is the one who would picture the scenario, as if I was a child in an adult body. See, it was my little self who was violated so it was my little self who needed to fight back.

Lindsey told me that pedophiles assault children without feeling guilty about their actions, and they often believe they are doing something good for the child. They easily remain in denial about the harm they cause and use ambiguous language to avoid the reality of seeing the abuse for what it is. She told me that, if I ever end up talking to Stringer, I have to use clear, concise language

- words that state exactly what occurred. Instead of saying, "you touched me when I was a kid" I would have to be more explicit, stating exactly what occurred. I hated that I might have to say that to him, thinking my word choices might arouse him. Even now, years later, it's disturbing to write about.

Talking about confrontations with Stringer was extremely uncomfortable but I felt safe in her presence, the Glock in her holster was certainly a factor. Of course, I cried a lot and puked a few times but we got through the process together, meeting several times during the spring to practice the different scenarios and it was during this time that I got up the courage to track him down, not knowing if he was still alive but hoping he was in prison.

Chapter Three

To my seemingly good fortune, my dad happened to fly into Oakland for a few hours on a business trip that spring. Because of his connections with the church, I was hopeful that he could assist me with my search for Stringer. As a youngster, he had been an altar boy and later entered the seminary. Sometime in the 1950's he met my mother and realized that the priesthood wasn't his calling... not just yet, anyway. He did, however, continue to participate in the church as an usher and an upstanding parishioner. At 6' 6" tall, he was handsome, took care of his physique and sported a thick mane of blonde hair that he kept clean, neat and parted to the side. Most everyone looked up to him, asked him for advice and assistance. People really liked my dad, they felt comfortable around him; he was easygoing and very funny. To the outsider, he was the perfect dad. Inside our home was a different story though and by the time I was 10, he had become an angry, violent and powerfully abusive alcoholic toward my mother, my sisters and myself. Healing that relationship over the years was an arduous task but well worth the effort.

I picked him up at the airport and we had dinner together in Jack London Square. I was not particularly close to my dad at that time but we had a shared interest in sobriety. He had been in AA for a number of years so we talked about meetings, caught up on family ties and then I brought up *the incident*. I asked him what he remembers of that time back in the late '60's/early '70's and although I don't recall exactly what he said, I know it wasn't much. Except for when he was causing violence in the home, dad wasn't a very present and conscious participant in our family by then, especially when it came to his children. He was the one I feared most but also the one I wished so much would protect me. Again, twisted pathology.

Because of that old craving for fatherly love that I had known the first 10 years of my life, I told my dad that I might start looking for Stringer and hoped he could help me with this. I even had daydreams of my dad going with me to confront Stringer. I thought that I needed another person to be there, to validate that part of the story and dad would be the perfect person. As if he could finally protect me from this monster child molester.

I pictured us at the front door and again, I see me as a child looking up at both my dad and Stringer. Like I was this small adult, it was the oddest thing. I never pictured me, grown-up C.M. actually speaking adult words and having an adult confrontation. Dad would finally be my hero!

Except it didn't work out as I had hoped. My dad didn't save the day. In fact, he did the opposite. He told me that if I just focused on the third step of the AA program and turned my will and my life over to a higher power, that I wouldn't have to involve Stringer in my process. That if I just focus on my own life, I wouldn't have to worry about anyone else, just keep my side of the street clean.

His comments brought me back to the telephone conversation I had several years prior with a priest friend of my mother named

Frank McClaren. I had been talking to my mom and asked her what happened after *it* had happened. Whom did I tell? What did I say? What was I told? Did anyone do anything? Did anyone care? My mother could not remember much about that time. She said that I told her right away, although this turned out not to be true. She also said that she went right to Frank McClaren and told him everything and that McClaren forced Stringer out of the church. This also wasn't true but it certainly was annoying that my own mother (and father) could not remember what occurred when Stringer, who was their close friend and parish priest, molested their daughter.

My mother had suggested that I call McClaren to get the rest of the story, fill in the blanks. She was still in contact with this priest and gave me his number. Reluctantly, I called McClaren and asked him what he remembers of *the incident*, which is how I still referred to the abuse at that time since I did not yet 'own' the vocabulary I use now. McClaren told me that he had not yet worked at our church, Claretville Seminary in 1970, but that he arrived years later. He said, "However, I recall your my mother telling me recently about that issue and that, you know, it was such a long time ago... it's water under the bridge... God forgives all people... if you just pray... you don't need to destroy his life..." and his verbiage faded away as I slowly set the receiver on its cradle.

I was shocked, paralyzed with disgust but baffled at why I thought I could possibly trust him, just another brother of that religious order. I thought to myself, "He's a jerk... but I'm an idiot." My self-esteem was still so low at that time. I felt no worth for my life; burdened with years of shame and complex guilt prescribed by those I trusted most. It was so difficult to unravel the twisted cords of confusion; I had spent my life trusting everyone but myself.

So there I was, having dinner with my dad, asking him the same thing and getting the same results. He did not support the idea of my search for Stringer. He thought it foolish and unnecessary which made me wonder at what he was hiding. Maybe it was guilt and remorse for not preventing all the abuse, molestations, and perverted behaviors that went on in and out of the home. Maybe he truly believed what he was saying. The irony of his words will be seen later in this story but suffice it to say, he found his way back to doing the right thing. After I dropped him off at the airport, sadness and anger were tumbling around inside of me. He betrayed me once again and that's when I stopped talking to my dad for about five years. Soon after, I changed my full name. With that small thread of connection now completely severed, I wanted to rid myself of his name and take my own. I went about the process in humble pursuit, trying on different names to see what worked. C.M. Morgan was perfectly tailored and fit just right. I have never regretted that decision.

At first I didn't miss him at all, there hadn't been much to miss in the past 15 years. But the memories of the first 10 years were pretty good and I began to miss the idea of that long ago dad. One of my sisters tirelessly pleaded for me to heal the relationship but there was nothing I could do. I knew it would take two of us to find our way back to a healthy father-daughter relationship and I didn't see it in either of us. Not yet, anyway.

It was up to me to find Stringer; I would have to do this alone. I had no idea how to go about finding this man, so the first thing I did was dial directory assistance to get the phone number of the Roman Catholic Archdiocese of Los Angeles. Then, I just went ahead and called the main number, not knowing what I would say, no script in mind and a woman answered the phone on the first ring. There were no automatic recordings at that time instructing us to "dial 1 for pedophiles, 2 for hypocrites, 3 for homophobes" etc. This very nice voice asked how could she help me, and numerous options ran through my mind, but out of my mouth came something like this:

Hello. I am looking for an old friend of mine, a close friend of the family named Bill Stringer. He was a priest at our church many years ago and I'm not even sure if he is still alive, but I'm wondering if you have any idea how I can find him.

She was happy to help me, put the receiver down on the wooden desk and I heard her walk through her office, open a file drawer and then a minute later she was back saying that yes, she does have his contact information. She told me he was no longer a priest but still receives the monthly diocese newsletter. She asked if I wanted to give her my name and number and pass it along to him. By now I was trembling with fear, my mouth was dry, my stomach sour. He was still alive.

No. No, uhhhhh… I actually want to surprise him. I would love for you to pass this message along to him but it would ruin the surprise. Ummmm… see, my family and I will be traveling soon and we want to pay him a visit, he was such a close friend…

And then she did it. She actually gave me his address and phone number. She sounded so happy to be of service, I could practically hear her smiling. Of course, that would never happen today but this was many years before societal awareness of clergy sex abuse. As I wrote down the contact details of the priest who had violated me as a child, I was stunned when she told me the city and state. He lived in Seattle. Seattle? I already had plans to visit Seattle in just a few months! I could barely believe it. Barely.

I thanked her kindly, hung up the phone and cried. I just cried for a while and I didn't know why. The next few months involved many good conversations with Maggie, my AA pals, another meeting with Lindsey and a phone call to the residence of one Benjamin Stringer. After a few rings, a woman answered the phone, she sounded like she could have been in her 60's. He lived with a woman.

"Hello?"

"Uhhh, hi there. I'm looking for Ben, is he around?"

"Yes he sure is, just a second..."

"Oh ummm, before you get him, I just want to make sure I have the right guy. I'm looking for an old friend of the family, Ben Stringer. He used to be a priest at our church, is this that same Ben?

"Oh yes it sure is. I'm sure he'd be happy to hear from you, one moment while I get him."

I heard her put a receiver down, heard her footsteps fade away as she called out, "Ben? Phone for you..." Then I set my index finger on the buttons and quietly disconnected the call. It was him!

When I bought the ticket to Seattle, Maggie was already working on one of the islands off shore so I had to schedule my flights according to her work schedule. She would have to take a ferry to the mainland in order to meet me at the airport.

Purchasing a plane ticket was very different in 1988 than it is now. There were no laptops to search for flights and compare airlines and fares. Everything was processed on the home telephone, calling different airlines, writing down all the information by hand. It was a time consuming process and although I do not remember details, I remember the feelings while going through the motions.

My heart pounding, my chest heavy as I spoke with the booking agent to make travel plans. A few days later, the tickets arrived in the mail. The original purpose for my visit had changed; it was no longer just about playing with my pal for a week in Seattle. Now I was going to confront a man who sexually abused me as a child. I was going face-to-face with a pedophile. The barrage of questions came pouring into my head. Is this really a good idea? Will I get caught? Would I actually get the opportunity to talk to Stringer? And what would I say if I met him? Am I still angry? Am I scared? What did I want to get out of this? Who does this kind of thing?

I could hear the voices of McClaren and my dad telling me to stand down, disapproving the very actions I was about to undertake. I could also hear the voices of Lindsey, my Sisters in Sobriety and all the therapists from the past few years supporting my desire to stand up for myself. My head was constantly in two-minds about this trip but my soul was set on fearless mode. This caused a great amount of confusion, doubt, and finally, awe of my inner self so brave and unwavering. I learned an important message back then: the soul always knows what's right at the time; shift into autopilot and keep my higher self at the helm. My ego ran for the toilet.

So the day came. My friend Julia took me to the airport in her green, well-kept, VW bus with Jinx the Border Collie at her side. Not yet a traveler, I had an old borrowed suitcase filled with the usual, plus a box of "brave cookies" that someone from the meetings baked for me to help me stay the course. For some reason that I can no longer recall, we were running late. There were no security lines back then so getting to the airport just in time was not a big deal.

However, I arrived to the airport too late. I missed my plane! One of the most important flights in my life and I wasn't on board. My heart sank to my shoes. Maybe they were right, maybe this is the universe telling me to back off and leave it be. Dejected, I turned to go back outside but Julia had already left the curb. So I shifted, once again into autopilot and I walked toward the ticketing area. The scene was almost surreal - there was hardly anyone else in the immediate area, no line to stand in and only one ticket agent at the counter. As I approached the desk, my eyes began to tear up. I was overcome with guilt, grief and anger at myself not to mention confusion about the supposedly amazing universe. Why did I miss this flight??

Once at the counter, I handed my now invalid ticket to an angel who, that day, was disguised as a ticket agent. She saw my tears and asked, with genuine concern, why I was so sad. I told her about the important journey I was on and actually said that I was going to find and confront my perpetrator, a priest who violated me when I was a child. I don't know what compelled me to tell her this too-much-information-but-still-the-truth of why I was so distraught. But I did and I remember that she had this soft, gentle smile while she told me how brave I was to do this. She also said that there was a problem with the reservation and that the ticket I had held was incorrect. Apparently, a mistake had been made on my original reservation and I was actually booked on the next flight to Seattle, which was leaving in a two hours. That is truly what happened and I just stood there, looking at her as if she knew something I didn't. As if we were both supposed to be there at that moment and her *real* job that day was to reassure me that all was in order.

I thanked her with my voice, but hugged her with my eyes! I was soon to realize the importance of having missed that first flight. Timing truly is everything.

Chapter Four

We didn't have a plan, Maggie and I. We had not booked a hotel room nor were we at all familiar with Seattle. Mags had a company car, I had an address and that was it. For some reason, we had not even discussed any kind of schedule for the next few days.

I realize that I often use the term "for some reason" but hindsight knows best. As is life, events often occur not for *some* reason, but for a *very important* reason, for the next event to occur so that the event after that can occur as well. If anything were different, everything would be different.

I digress… back to Seattle. As it happens, Maggie had also been running late, she had missed her ferry and without cell phones, we had no way of knowing that we would both arrive at the airport late, but as it turned out, perfectly on time. We were happy to see each other and pulled off at the nearest pay phone to check the yellow pages for something familiar. We looked under Bed & Breakfast, Gay bar, and Lesbian bookstore, anything that felt welcoming, familiar and/or accommodating. We drove to a Gay bar to hopefully inquire of any gay-owned B&B's but the place was closed. The next stop was a place called the Wild Rose Café in downtown Seattle and as usual, I could not have predicted the magic that was about to happen.

Walking into the Wild Rose was like walking into the 1970's; it was a Lesbian owned bookstore, café and bar all wrapped into one. Flyers on the windows announcing Tuesday's open Mic, that summer's music festivals and Cris Williamson in concert. Passing through the old, wooden doors, we entered directly into the bar with a wide opening on the left to the small bookstore and reading room. Well-worn wood floors, tables and chairs were scattered throughout, a rack in the corner held political newspapers and local gay rags. A bulletin board with an assortment of more flyers announcing past and future poetry recitals, political gatherings, index cards with "for-sale" items, and half sheets of "looking for roommate" scattered throughout. Around the room were posters touting rainbow flags and Pride marches, inducements to boycott Coor's beer and one of my favorites, the poster with a photo of two gorgeous butch womyn in a delicious moment of intimacy and the words "Power Breakfast" written below them in 72 point font. Another sign that all is right, I am where I am supposed to be.

There were very few women inside, no one in the bookstore café section and we sat at the bar. I was sober at the time so sitting at a bar was not the norm for me. However, the environment was familiar and welcoming, as was the bartender. After checking in with me to make sure I was comfortable (which was unnecessary but so very thoughtful) Maggie ordered a beer and I got a coke soda. We picked up a few local papers and began looking through them for a gay-owned someplace to stay. We were having fun looking at all the local flavors, forgetting for a moment the 'other' reason for my visit. I was so happy to be doing this with Maggie; we always had so much fun together. I could not have chosen a more perfect soldier with whom to share this foxhole.

The angel, now disguised as a bartender named Barbara, noticed we were not locals and that's when it started. It being the magic, remember? She was friendly and clearly wise, older and extremely kind. She asked where we were from, what we were looking for and why we were in town. She did not need to make conversation, there was plenty of busy work for her to do, but she was sincere in wanting to know about our path.

By this time, there were only four of us in the room - Barbara, Maggie, myself and yet another angel disguised as yet another woman in the world who sat a few stools to my right. As we conversed with Barbara, the other woman, Janie, couldn't help but listen in and this is about how the conversation went, beginning with the answer to what we were looking for:

ME: So yeah... we're looking for a place to stay for a few nights, preferable a gay-owned B&B.

BARBARA: Oh yeah well there's a few around; I can point you in the right direction. What brings you to Seattle?

(Maggie was painfully shy to most of the rest of the world, which I found endearing, so as usual; I did most of the talking)

ME: Well... the main reason I'm here is because I'm looking for a perpetrator, a priest who sexually violated me when I was a kid. I found out he was living here in Seattle so I want to find him and talk to him about it. About what happened.

Janie puts down her newspaper and looks our way.

BARBARA: Really? Wow... that's brave.

I was being called brave a lot during that time. I liked being called brave, it was like I was a hero. In retrospect, I see that I truly was becoming my own hero.

BARBARA: What is it you want to accomplish? Ya gonna kill him?

JANIE: (with a sly grin) Need some help with that?

ME: Yeah, I might… need some help, anyway. No I don't plan to kill him… I don't even know if I'm going to find him but I'm gonna try. I'm not totally sure exactly what I want from this; I just know I have to do it.

BARBARA: Well, it's good to maybe come up with some goals here. I work part-time in a clinic for abused and battered women. I've worked with a lot of women who want to confront their perps, the outcomes are always so varied, you never know what they're going to do, how they're going to react. They usually deny it.

JANIE: Mine did. I confronted my uncle not too long ago and he denied the whole thing. Called ME a liar, my family didn't support me either. I'm sure he messed with my sister, too, but no one will talk about it, no one will deal with it. It was a crappy experience but that was mine, hopefully you might have a different one.

BARBARA: Just remember to use the real words. Say what it is that happened. Pedophiles keep their secrets from everyone else including themselves by denying the violence and glossing over the actions.

I... I just really could barely believe this moment in time. I kept looking at Barbara, then to Janie then to Maggie then back to Barbara, cycling through my wonder of this perfect union of, and total reverence for... us. All four of us were honored to be there, right then, at that moment, that day. There, in The Wild Rose Café.

Chapter Five

Winter 2012 — Minneapolis, MN

It's called clergy abuse. Alive and well, it thrives as its own peculiar culture in many religions. Culture is the collective awareness of knowledge, values, attitudes, beliefs and roles acquired by a group of people in the course of generations through individual and group striving. Culture is passed along by communication and imitation from one generation to the next. It is a way of life, systems of knowledge shared by a relatively large group of people; behavioral norms proceed generally without anyone thinking about them. Cultures contains patterns of acquired behavior and the collective programming of individuals therein. So again, it's called clergy abuse. Alive and well, it thrives as its own peculiar culture in many religions.

Horrific in-breeding of this dark, deeply secretive culture, survives in the lives of thousands, perhaps millions, wrapped up in one neat phrase with two small words; clergy abuse. We see it on the headline; we hear it on the news. *"Oh, sure, I read about that. It's clergy abuse,"* I've heard people say this phrase, as if it is a normal topic. It's a misnomer, isn't it? Clergy abuse - as if there is abuse of and toward the clergy.

It's actually abuse perpetrated towards minors by members of the collar and surprisingly, many people don't even believe it happens. I've watched them on the evening news - the faithful followers and most prideful pious - protesting with signs stating that the victims of clergy abuse are lying; That the real victims are the clergy themselves and of course, it's the parishioners who suffer as well. I laugh when I think about them spewing such sordid rhetoric about people they never met lying about something they know nothing about while wearing their WWJD lanyards. Their ignorance shines brilliant.

The term 'clergy abuse' came into my awareness in 2002. The non-profit support group for survivors of clergy sexual abuse, Survivors Network of those Abused by Priests (SNAP), had been advocating for a law in California that lifted the statute of limitations for one full year on child sexual abuse cases perpetrated by the clergy. An attorney who had represented over 300 plaintiffs in clergy abuse cases drafted the legislation. The lifting of the statute of limitations allowed hundreds of attorneys to file thousands of new lawsuits throughout every county in California. This was huge and it was also the first real public acknowledgement of this widespread abuse in the country.

Important to note here that there are hundreds of articles and supporting facts highlighting the surprising amount of angry backlash and anger towards victims caused by this law. One great example comes from the Catholic League for Religious and Civil Rights, also referred to as the Catholic Leagues, it is an American Catholic anti-defamation and civil rights organization. This organization is reported to have criticized SNAP by calling it a phony victims' group.

Phony? Unfortunately, we will never know all of the facts - numerous victims have stayed silent and hundreds of others have passed away, some from documented suicide due to the abuse. According to numerous watchdog organizations, attorneys, court files and press reports, here are just a few of the facts: Between 1984-2010, several thousand lawsuits have been filed throughout the United States and over $3 Billion in awards and settlements have been made. In Los Angeles alone, approximately 77% of the parishes have had pedarest accusations filed against them in court; fewer than 2 percent of sexual abuse allegations against the Catholic Church appear to be false; Nationwide, nineteen bishops in the U.S. have been accused of sexual abuse, approximately 6,115 priests have been accused of sexual abuse and a total of 16,324 victims had come forward with allegations. The public was finally beginning to realize that cases of abuse were commonplace in the Catholics Churches.

Many other lawsuits have been filed against members of the Catholic hierarchy because they did not report sex abuse allegations to local and legal authorities. Factual court evidence has shown that these self-declared religious men deliberately moved sexually abusive priests to other parishes where the abuse often continued. I'm not making this up. This is far from phony. In 2002, approximately two-thirds of sitting U.S. bishops were alleged to have knowingly kept accused priests in ministry or moved accused priests to new assignments. The results made public in 2004 showed that even after the public outcry, priests were moved out of the country but were placed in environments which brought them into contact with children, despite church claims to the contrary.

The National Conference of Catholic Bishops claims it does not keep statistics on these civil or criminal suits. Hmmm, why is that? According to Pope Benedict XVI, Catholic social teaching "is simply to help purify reason and to contribute, here and now, to the acknowledgment and attainment of what is just." The hypocrisy is almost too much to think about.

Catholic parishioners were given conflicting bits of information at mass as to how the new law will effect the church and many people chose to stay uninformed. Adding insult to injury, many of them called us liars, handed out flyers in front of churches protesting the victim's accusations. People held rallies to support the accused priests. As of this writing, court cases of clergy sexual abuse are still being filed throughout the country. The Catholic Archdiocese of Minneapolis, St. Paul and other Minnesota towns are currently under serious investigation for their roles in clergy sexual abuse with minor children. Even the police chief of St. Paul has reported in the media that archdiocese officials have not been cooperating on the priest sex abuse cases. Yet still, parishioners attend church every Sunday, putting their hard-earned money into the baskets.

In 2003, I met Joseph Stanley, the attorney who was to represent me throughout the next five years of litigation against the Roman Catholic Archdiocese of Los Angeles. Clergy Abuse. I don't really like the term, obviously. I prefer to call it something more along the lines of "vile sexual abuse of children perpetrated by pedophiles who hide under the hoax of religious reverence." However, that barely scratches the surface of the pain caused by this crime termed 'clergy abuse.'

When I go there, to that pain, sometimes accidentally, sometimes on purpose - either from an inner or outer stimuli - hundreds of thought bubbles emerge and float around my head, filled with scenes from personal to global. So numerous, they suspend my being for any length of time, then I lose the moment to a particle of the past. It's not unlike one of those autumn days in the big mid-west when it's super sunny outside. Enjoying the warmth you notice a bit of shadow leading your gait and then looking up you see them; miles of huge, fluffy white clouds way, way up there, threatening to block the beauty, the heat of the moment. So I stop looking and keep walking. But I know the clouds are still there.

My folks, Lawrence and Ann were raised in the conundrum of Catholicism; the 'control the masses via weekly masses' theory of morality management. They had four daughters and religiously indoctrinated us into the church of ironic indolence. Every Sunday, we were there. It started when I was very young; my first eight years were spent in Howard Beach, New York. I attended 1st - 3rd grade at St. Helen's Catholic School, the building securely attached to the church so that no one could stray too far from the canon. I did not like the rigidity of Catholic school and even at that early age, I was intuitively uncomfortable with the priests. However, I loved my uniform - no surprise there - and my fondest memories are of my first grade teacher, Sister Maureen. She was friendly, compassionate and fun! She cared about me, talked to me, asked me why I chewed-up all my pencils. My worst encounters were with Henry Brogan. They called him father Brogan, but for this book, I refuse to use to the more colloquial term of the capitalized "F" of father. I refuse to subscribe to their self-appointed, aggrandized entitlements.

As churchgoers, my parents were involved with the congregation, especially my mom. She loved the priests and seminarians and apparently could not get enough of them to save her soul. She often had them over at our house for most of my childhood. Dinners, holidays, parties, a celebration of any kind and Brogan was there for all of them. I believe he was the first to violate my sisters and I. He was tall, rugged, egotistical and condescending. He was mean, grabbing us to him, forcing us onto his lap and "tickling" us until we cried in pain. I hated him. My mother watched uncomfortably but trusted that 'the father' knew what he was doing. I don't know where my dad was during these times but I imagine Brogan waited until dad was out of sight.

Parents love seeing their children with their priests. It's in the culture of religion to blindly trust those in authority, no matter what your own guts are telling you. No matter that you see your own child in utter discomfort at the hands of a man whom you really know nothing about except that he recites your liturgy and enjoys a good meatloaf. This man who chooses to allegedly maintain celibacy... and the flocks believe every last word. It is a sadly unfortunate truth for many children born into the religious cultures. It's a sacrament of sadism.

I despised Brogan, even more so when I had to attend confession. Think about this for a moment... what can a seven year old possibly confess to a man who abuses her? That she is guilty of innocence? The irony here is of a precious sort and you can see how the twisted dogma begins to tighten and smother our wee perfect souls.

Gratefully, my family left NY in 1968. Dad had been working for a large company and got a job transfer to Thousand Oaks, California, a sprawling city one hour north of Los Angeles. This had been a major victory for dad who had been a serious alcoholic with lousy job retention... redundant, I know. As it turned out, he lost that job several years later but by then, we were firmly planted on the Left Coast, never to return to the repression of the New York suburbs.

So I was about eight years old when we moved and two years later, my parents discovered Claretville Seminary and that's where we met Bill Stringer, a priest under the Claretian order. The Catholics have such a complicated system of orders and hierarchies. Ordinary humans are given extraordinary titles such as "Supreme Pontiff" and "Holy See." I wonder about people who have an irascible need for such unearthly titles.

Housed at Claretville from 1952-1977 were The Claretians, a community of Roman Catholic priests and seminarians with

29

a "special devotion to the Blessed Virgin Mary." I know some people see this as a normal reality, but now healthy is this? Adult men who supposedly do not want to engage in intimacy with a female adult, but they are devoted to woman who has been dead for centuries. Add to this their obsession of female virginity and I'm sure there is some diagnosis listed in the Physician's Desk Reference by the American Psychological Association and if there isn't, there certainly should be.

Claretville was located in Calabasas, at the intersection of Mulholland Highway and Las Virgenes Canyon Road in the Santa Monica Mountain Range and had been the former Gillette Ranch Estate in Calabasas. It was a beautiful park-like environment complete with a small lake that we jumped into from a swinging rope knotted on a giant Oak tree. I'll never forget the Gillette razor blade-shaped pool located near the tennis courts amidst the 588 sprawling acres. The Claretians sold the property in 1978 and it is now part of Malibu Creek State Park.

My family attended church every Sunday at Claretville Seminary for about eight years and amidst the chaos and abuse at home and church, there truly were some great memories at Claretville. The service was hip and cool, unorthodox and even eccentric at times. A very progressive church, it was the polar opposite of the mass we had attended in New York. Claretville had a rockin' 5-piece band complete with electric guitar, bass and drum set. The Peace-Time interlude lasted a half hour while everyone visited with each other and the band played songs from the soundtrack, "Godspell" and "Jesus Christ Superstar." It was fun, at first and I had looked forward to seeing my new community every Sunday morning.

Much to my father's chagrin, my mother continued to surround herself and our family with these clergymen. Like so many others, she trusted them inherently; they were always in our home.

It was the early '70's when the priests decided to turn around and face the people, unwillingly, I imagine. *Ad Orientum*, the liturgical norm for 18 centuries, was the old custom in which the priest did not face the people, but only faces the altar. Well that's convenient! So many layers of sardonicism right there in that old norm. Sardonic, you might ask? One dictionary describes 'sardonic' as, "... alluding to a Sardinian plant which, when eaten, was supposed to produce convulsive laughter ending in death." Oh perfect.

However by 1965, the Second Vatican Council instituted the more human approach of actually facing their congregation. I reckon the pederasts were both frightened and thrilled with this new policy; although they had to face those they violated, they could also prolong their ritualistic perve-sessions while providing their spiritualistic Sunday sessions. Two birds, one stone. I can only imagine that this also made it easier for them to choose their next victims. Three birds, I guess.

—⁓∿∘◠◡◯◠◡∘◠∿⁓—

Abuse can do weird things to a child's brain. For me, time past is distorted; places and people are mixed up with each other. What I thought happened at one time actually happened at another. My mind tried to take care of my soul and for many years into my adulthood, I had thought that the sexual abuse from Stringer in particular began when I was about eight years old. It wasn't until I decided to file a lawsuit that I realized I was closer to age 10, which unfortunately, added yet another layer of guilt. *You think by ten I would have known better!* That's how I still treated myself at the time, as if it was still my fault. Now when I see a ten-year-old girl, it's clear to me that ten-years-old is still pretty tiny. Ten should not be touched.

Chapter Six

Back to the Wild Rose Café. Bonded in our courage to face those who have harmed us, brought fatefully together as if we were connecting pieces in our own private puzzle, we embraced each other as chosen family. We talked in depth about the pros and cons when facing our perpetrators; the fears, the strengths, the unknowns of the moment when you actually see them again. One thing was clear - that no matter what the perps say or do, confronting them is always empowering... if you are ready. It reminds me of the time I ran the Honolulu Marathon in 2005. It would not have mattered if I didn't finish. The important parts were the lessons and strength gained from the training. When I got the to starting line, I felt like a champ!

We talked for a while longer, the conversation ended on an upbeat and powerful note. Barbara sent us off with the best of vibes and I have never seen her since but the impact of her wisdom stayed with me. She may never know how she affected my path, but it's a good reminder for us all to know that we can deeply touch each other while doing the mundane chores of life.

Janie had invited us to stay with her for a few days. We had only known this womon for two hours but the pact was made and the trust was certain. The three of us headed to Janie's house, winding through the streets of Seattle, me on the back of Janie's motorcycle with Maggie following in her car. Ten minutes later, we arrived at her small, two-bedroom bungalow on a quiet street somewhere in Seattle. Janie lived alone and our guest room doubled as her office/closet/catch-all space and there was a comfortable bed there for us to rest at night.

What a blessing, having been granted the comforts of home rather than the indifferent cube of a hotel room. Janie's place had spiritual sayings on the walls, women-made art, feminist stickers on the fridge and of course, plenty of herbal tea. I felt cradled in the power of female, in the strength of courageous women who have walked before me, confronting all the shit we dare to defy.

We chatted for a bit, the three of us, and then we opened a map of Seattle on the old, yellow laminated kitchen table. Janie pointed out her home, "you are here" and I unfolded the piece of paper with the details I had come to know as a destination from determination: Stringer's home address.

Unlike today's technology, GPS screens and swipes, we had to physically flip the large map over, find the street name in the alphabetical columns, jot down the letter and number coordinates, flip the map back over and pin point our location. With my left index finger on Janie's home, my right hand moved down the letter column and over the numbered rows and... there it was. My index fingers were merely six inches apart. We were but half a foot from my perpetrator. He lived about 15 minutes from Janie's home! What???

How do I describe *these* feelings? Layers of excitement in a not-so-joyful way; courage & fear daring each other to stay out in front, lead the pack. In my own private world, I was a crew of one body, many souls and a myriad of thoughts. My mouth dries, my body sweats, my head is hot and my feet are cold. I want to laugh and cry, dance and vomit. At first I don't do anything, then a shiver runs cold up my shoulders into my neck. I am 20 years and fifteen minutes away from someone who caused so much hurt, so much confusion and years of unresolved angst. I am six inches from confronting the catholic disgrace and hypocrisy that races and rages throughout the lives of the vulnerable and the small and I wanted them all with me. All the victims of this horror, thousands, possibly millions since forever ago, I wanted them to be in the kitchen with us. I wanted to point to the map and tell them, "Okay, we'll start here, all of us, right here in the middle of Seattle and then work our way out until we find them all. Yours and yours and yours until we are all sated with eternal justice."

We charted the best route on the map and I wrote down the directions. Janie had to head off for work, Maggie and I remained at her home and stayed close to each other. She was my rock solid friend that weekend, selfless and superb in her support. All set for the next day, the big day, we decided that we would awaken whenever without an alarm clock, find coffee and track down Stringer. I cried then laughed, puked then danced… in that order. I felt everything, especially anxiety. Would he be there? Who would answer the door? Will I survive? I barely slept that night, my mind suspended in busy brain syndrome, "BBS" as my sister calls it.

The sun did rise the next morning and I awoke in a dream-like state of emotional strength. I was ready, not scared, nervous but no longer anxious. We showered, dressed and the thought occurred to me: What should I wear? What does one wear in this situation? Steel-toed boots came to mind along with some spiritual under armor and a flak jacket, just in case. I could have started a clothing line, "Face-the Perp" fashion outfits. Instead, I went for absolute comfort and wore my usual Levi 501's, a long sleeve pull over shirt and hiking boots, regular toe. A few precious stones from friends went into my pockets along with other tiny trinkets of luck and love.

With Maggie behind the wheel, we found some coffee and donuts, the breakfast of champions! Then we followed the directions on the neatly folded piece of lined paper. It was around 10:00 AM by now; we drove a couple of miles down Hwy 90 and a few streets over. It was a quiet, fairly poor part of town. One last right turn and a half a block down we slowed and drove by a long, wide alley. As we passed, I saw his numbers on a two story a few houses away.

"Let's go around the block again," I said to Maggie. She drove slowly as we talked about how I was feeling, thinking and how I wanted to proceed. We decided that Maggie would park on the street just past the alley driveway but in clear sightline of Stringer's house. I would go alone, at first. I had to do this part alone. It was as if my adult self had to show my inner, long forgotten, ignored child self that I would take care of her. I would do the fighting now. Finally, someone was going to protect her and that someone was adult me. Maggie parked the truck, we said a few words, hugged and I opened the car door. I told her that if he was there, I would first see if I could get him out of the house, go for a walk and talk with me. If I needed or wanted her, she would know it.

I think back on that time, on how Maggie must have felt. What was that like for her, to sit there as I went to face my perpetrator? It had been several years since we had talked last. So I called her...

Great conversation! Although we hadn't spoken in years, it was like we never lost touch. We started with audio on the mobile phone, and then realizing we both had smart phones, we switched to video. Mags looked great; it was so good to see her, I wanted to give her a huge hug but alas, technology brings us together while it keeps us apart. I was grateful that we had video, that we were both alive and well after all the years. Good memories floated by as we caught up to the present by reliving the past. We have both aged, of course, and I had forgotten this until I saw both Maggie and my own self-view. We have jowls now. Although small but visible, they're just getting started on their way heading south. We have some grey hairs and more wisdom in our eyes. Our convo was lively, back & forth, non-stop. No awkward moments looking for things to say.

When I had asked about her experience of that time in Seattle, how it was for her to be there with me, her response surprised me. "I was totally honored, like I mattered enough to you that you wanted me there. It was special, I felt special, I felt like a hero, doing the right thing. I felt fearless, standing up for those who have been wronged. It was important for me to be there for you." Again, sometimes we don't know how our path affects others and this was one of those times. We were two Amazon warriors in a tiny battle, side by side in the foxhole, facing an enemy of my childhood. This was my conflict, but our combat. This had been my struggle but our surge. Our love and respect for each other was the gear I had needed at that time to protect myself from the unknown of what had happened next. Her fearlessness was my helmet; her support was my army. We probably could have talked all night and into the dawn, I missed her lots. But we both had to be up early in the morning so we said our goodbyes and pledged to stay in touch.

I walked up the wide, trash-strewn alley. The houses were old, had not been cared for and were all spaced one lot apart from each other. This was a run-down neighborhood, no manicured lawns, and no well-intentioned architecture; just buildings slapped together for shelter with as few windows as possible. I walked by one house on the left, and then saw his home up ahead; the second on the right, about a one-minute walk away. Front doors facing the back alley, apartment B was up a long flight of stairs on the second story. Looking back one more time at Mags and taking a deep breath, I walked down a short, dirt driveway and ascended the 15 wooden, rickety steps. Reaching the top stair, I silently asked for strength and sent out my gratitude. Then I knocked on the dirty, paint peeled door.

A young boy of about seven opened the door slightly, peering up at me and brushing his longish hair away from his eyes. He didn't say anything so I began to speak the words announcing today's event. Smiling, I said to the boy, "Hey there! I'm looking for Bill Stringer, is he home?" The boy turned and yelled out, "Daaaaad! Someone's at the door for you."

Dad? Had the pedophile priest become a pedophile father? A lateral move I suppose, however I was shocked because I had not imagined his life after the church laicized him back in the 70's. I knew he lived in Seattle and a woman had answered his phone, but kids? Dad?

The boy turned away, the door closed slightly and I froze. Then the door opened again and thus appeared in the threshold a short, balding, pudgy, pale man with glasses. He looked up at me and asked, "Can I help you?" I told him I was looking for Bill Stringer. He confirmed that was him, then asked again if he could help me.

Help me? I had to laugh to myself and thought, "in a moment you're the one who'll be needing help".

37

Chapter Seven

In the years leading up to this event, all the talking, thinking, researching & rehearsing I had done, the reality of aging and growing up had escaped me. He got shorter and I had grown much taller since I had last seen him when I was a kid. Now, at 5' 10" tall, I had a good five inches over this... this person who up until that moment had been such a scary memory but was now just an old, white, balding, pasty-faced loser. He had not taken very good care of himself. Karma, I suppose.

"My name is C.M. Morgan. When you were a priest at Claretville, you were good friends with my parents, Larry & Ann Morgan. Remember them?"

He looked down as if in deep thought, but I think he knew right away and did not really know what to do except to look down as if in deep thought.

"Oh yes, I think so. Would you like to come in?"

*You **think** so? You think you might remember the life you distorted?*

"No, I would like you to come out and talk with me about what happened when I was a kid, what you did to me when I was just ten years old. You know what I'm talking about."

"Oh, uhhhh… well, yes okay. Look, we're throwing a surprise birthday party for one of my sons this afternoon. My wife is out shopping right now. Can you come back later?"

Speaking of surprises, "Nope. I'm here now. We need to talk about this now."

"Okay, okay I see. Okay then, ahhhh… let me tell my sons that I need to leave for a bit. I'll be right back."

He closed the door, but I wedged my foot in close to stop it from latching into the frame. So there I stood, hearing Stringer talk to his kids although I couldn't make out the words. I look back now and wonder what was going through his mind. He had no way of knowing if I was there alone or if I had someone waiting in a get-away car with a .45 pointed at his temples. I also wondered if his kids were old enough to care for themselves. Was it okay for him to leave them alone? Did he molest them, too?

I wasn't scared as I waited although I probably should have been. I really did not know this man. Would he come to the door holding a gun? Was he calling the police? Was anyone else besides Maggie watching this? I didn't have the answers, but my soul was at peace. I was calm and in control of this situation. This time, his fate was in my hands.

After a few minutes, he came to the door, looked up at me and asked me again what I wanted. I told him I wanted to go for a walk and talk about what he did to me when I was ten years old. He nodded, shut the dirty door behind him and then we started down the wooden, rickety steps. I followed him, then we walked side-by-side over the dirt driveway and back up the alley from whence I came. His gait was slow; he was old now and not too healthy. Right away, I couldn't help but feel empowered, he was so short and… and dumb looking.

I started out by saying, "Do you remember who I am?" and he did. He knew why I was there.

———⁓⁓⚬⚬⚬⚬⚬⚬⚬⚬⚬⚬⚬———

One of the more vivid incidents occurred upstairs in my parent's bedroom, while the party continued below. It was a party like all the other ones they had - lots of priests, seminarians, parishioners and alcohol. Apparently, Stringer told my folks that he would tuck me into bed that night. Although I do not remember entering my parent's bedroom, I clearly remember everything else that happened that night. As a child, of course I trusted him but I knew that what he was doing was wrong, very wrong. For the sake of this book, I cannot describe what took place. However, the fact that the "gentle tickling" part felt good was so confusing to my little mind. Soon there after, I could only stare at the objects in my parent's bedroom. Looking back, I have no recollection of what my own room looked like but I can easily recall, to this day, the placement of my parent's television stand, the dresser drawers and the mirror, the sliding glass doors leading to the patio and the paintings on the walls. I had to mentally check out to survive the sexual and emotional abuse that was taking place. This mechanism served me well several other times in my childhood and up through my teenage years.

———⁓⁓⚬⚬⚬⚬⚬⚬⚬⚬⚬⚬⚬———

Back to Seattle, it was 1988, I was 28 years old and doing the unthinkable. Facing my abuser as an adult and I spoke to him, with assertive defiance, the words that I had practiced so many times and the conversation went something like this:

"So what the hell?!" I could feel my anger rise to the surface. "You sexually abused me when I was just ten years old! Several times!" I spoke the descriptive words I had practiced so many times and then asked him, "What actually happened after that, where did you go and what are you doing with kids in your house?"

He was looking down as he started to answer so I interrupted, tapped him on the shoulder with the back of my hand and told him to look at me. I needed to see his eyes and I wanted him to see me, not just speak words to the air.

Through his thick, dirty glasses he answered, "Yes, well. After it was reported I was sent away for a while to New Mexico for some kind of rehabilitation. I knew I had a bad problem and shortly after that I was asked to leave the church."

Fast forward for a moment - in 2002, again before it all blew wide open, I had the good fortune of talking on the phone with another unsuspecting clergy staff at the L. A. Archdiocese. Again, prior to any awareness of maintaining privacy, the staff person read Stringer's file to me and informed me that Stringer had in fact been laicized after being sent away to a retreat near Jemez Springs, in New Mexico's Sangre de Cristo Mountains.

I had not yet known about "Camp Ped" (Google that!) and I had presumed that Stringer left the church on his own accord. This rehab center formally known as the "Father Fitzgerald Center" is operated by a little-known Roman Catholic religious order called the Holy Servants of the Paracletes. It was originally established in the late 1940's as a refuge for alcoholic and depressed priests with no place else to go. However, since the 1970's it has been a joke of a rehab center, also known as Camp Ped and is still in business today. Leaders in the Catholic Church had known for years that pedophilia could not be cured, so priests were sent there for a few weeks of fresh air where, as it was revealed in the court documents, they shared their secrets with each other and then were sent out again armed with more information on who had been where. The rehab center was thoroughly ill equipped to deal with pedophiles and there is plenty of public information to support this fact.

I was to later find out that, although he had asked to leave the church in 1973, three years after he sexually abused me, and the leave was granted, files show that Stringer's laicization happened not only because of accusations (which were never grounds to dismiss a priest anyway) but also because he had already gotten married! So basically, he got fired as he was trying to quit.

"I spent years in therapy" he told me "and although there is no cure for my illness, there are corrective measures, therapy and continued awareness. My wife knows about my past, she doesn't know names but she knows what happened. There were two other girls as well. My sons are from my wife's first marriage and we don't have any issues there. My illness was toward young girls, not boys."

By this time we turned onto the sidewalk, I gave Maggie the "I'm okay" sign as we walked a few more feet then I stopped and let my anger take the lead. I was so mad!

"Why? Why did you do that? Do you have any idea how your selfish, filthy behavior messed me up for so many years? Do you have any clue how many therapists I've seen, how crappy I have felt about myself? How dirty I have felt regarding sex and the impossible quest for any type of real, safe intimacy? Are you at all aware of the life long scars you have created?" I was almost but not quite yelling by this time. "I've been so angry with you, I hate you! I want you to feel the loneliness I have felt, the isolation, the doubt, the fears. I want you to feel it all. I never even knew if it was ever really real, I doubted myself so many times. Fuck you! Just, Fuck you!"

And he listened. He looked at me the whole time and listened. He didn't argue, he didn't deny. He just stayed quiet and listened. So I started walking again and as we headed toward the stop sign on the corner, it was his turn to talk.

"I'm... I'm so sorry. No, I did not know the depth of scars I had left but I have prayed for you and the other two most every day since I realized that what I had done was truly wrong. I've prayed that you would have forgotten the molestation and..."

"FORGOTTEN!! Are you kidding me? Do you seriously believe that? If you were so sorry, why didn't you ever do your homework and go look for me to apologize?"

"Well, no I don't believe that anyone could have forgotten something so horrible. I had thought of looking for you and the others in the years past, but I was scared that it might make things worse. So I have prayed for you. Prayed that you would grow past it, grow up healthy and I prayed for forgiveness. I hated myself for what I had done and I am so very, very sorry."

Again, he was looking up at me the whole time and I could feel his disgust with himself. I also felt his remorse. This I did not expect. Of all the scenes I had rehearsed, this had not been one of them.

By now we had turned around and were walking back down the sidewalk. I motioned for Maggie to come out of the truck. I wanted her to meet him, I needed a witness to see that he was real and I wanted him to see that I had a witness to this life-changing event.

I introduced them, Maggie laughed and said, "Ben! I've heard so much about you" and he bowed his head in absolute shame. Then he looked at me and apologized again, asking what he could ever possibly do to make amends. I told him, "I came here to get three things from you - First, validation in front of a witness that you did in fact sexually abuse me when you were a priest and I was only 10 years old. I also came here to get an apology from you and I'd like you to pay for half of my round trip airfare!"

Since then, many have asked me, "Half of the airfare and an apology? Is that all?" And my answer has always been yes, that's what I needed. It was so critical that he admitted his behavior, that he acknowledged it was wrong and that he apologized to me. The validation was deep and the apologies were thick with remorse. I had longed to know, to really know that I was telling the truth. Having Maggie there to see it and feel it, reassured me that this was real.

So he did it, in front of my best friend. He admitted his behavior to us both, stated it was horribly wrong and apologized again. Then he said, "I could try to pay for your whole airplane ticket but I might have to make a few payments. As you can see, we don't have much here. You could give me your address and... oh wait, you probably don't want me to have your address."

I laughed at that last line and told him, "Yes, I'll give you my address. I'm not scared of you anymore and I know where to find you if I need to."

So I gave him my address and we just stared at each other for a few moments. As Maggie started back into her car, he said, "Thank you" and I watched him turn and walk away. I didn't know what to do, how to end this. A few steps later, he turned to look at me, and walking slowly in a kind of sideways direction back to his house he spoke up in a louder tone, "Thank you! I'm sorry! Thank you for giving me this opportunity, thank you for letting me make amends. Thank you for coming here! You're amazing. I'm so sorry! You're a very brave woman!" and tears started to flow out from under his thick, dirty glasses.

His hands went up to the bridge of his nose, pushing his glasses up as he tried to redirect the flow of water running from his eyes. He turned and walked slowly toward his house, head bowed down.

I watched for another moment, then couldn't anymore and turned and got in the passenger seat. I was silent, shocked at what had just taken place. Maggie patiently waited, then said, "Where to?" and I went directly to my core. I was blown wide open and just began to cry, purging all that had been inside for so many years. I cried hard, feeling the pain but at the same time, I was so happy, so triumphant! I did it! I won! I was so very brave!

And I forgave. Slowly but certainly, forgiveness seeped deep into my soul. That, too, was entirely unexpected.

The next few hours are a blur but I do remember that eventually we got back to Janie's and told her the whole story. It was great to retell it, to have Maggie concur and have Janie cheer us on. As fate would have it, Janie told us that the Wellington sisters were playing a hometown concert of sorts for a bunch of womyn over on one of the islands. The Wellington's!?! I loved their music! They were well known as the original 'Godmothers of Chick Rock.' The stars were lined up just so perfectly and I could not have asked for a more healing way to end the day. We quickly drove to the pier, got the car on the ferry, picked up some of Janie's pals on the other side and headed into the woods. Arriving at someone's giant barn, out in the middle of seemingly nowhere, there they were - J&J Wellington. Sisters & singer-songwriters since the early '60's, who play rock, folk and many songs that touched me deep, helping to boost the healing process. They played a great show to about 100 womyn that night and we danced under the stars. The energy, the spark, the rhythm soothed and calmed my aches. Such magic in the world! Healing is always here.

The next day brought us to the softball field where the local women's league had a few games going on. There we sat, in the sun, watching all these women play the field. We had a great time and I was grateful for a most amazing weekend. I flew back home that evening and a few weeks later, I received a check from Stringer. As the months passed, I started to feel my self worth come back, the experience had made me stronger and I began to like, even love myself again. It was that pure love I was born with, that easy feeling of being.

Forgiveness - it has to be the lifeblood of all healing. In forgiving Stringer, I was able to see him as a true spirit inside an ill human body. I no longer saw a horrible man; I no longer hated him either. Whenever I tell this story, I deeply feel his longing for forgiveness. This is where we can all connect, if we look deep enough and stay there long enough, this is where the human condition meets its core, its beginning. Hopefully, we all learn at some point that forgiveness is the key to the knowledge of our truly connected selves. We are all one.

My dad and I eventually healed our relationship when he sent me a letter in 1993 that caught me off guard but taught me another lesson about forgiving. His letter was about regrets, about taking responsibility and asking for forgiveness. It was introspective and he acknowledged his part, which allowed me to acknowledge mine. Gratefully, I was receptive at his attempt for reconnection and I have never regretted taking this path.

After confronting Stringer, I thought that part of my life was laid to rest and that I had put the abuse in my past. Even though thoughts and feelings cropped up now and then, I thought I was pretty much done with any further actions in that direction... until 15 years later in 2002, when my dad called with a message that could not have come from anyone more perfect than he.

Chapter Eight

I was living in Oakland, CA and working as a Sign Language Interpreter, having switched career gears a few years back. I began to hear random reports on the car radio regarding clergy sexual abuse. Even though the issue of child sexual abuse by U.S. Catholic priests was first nationally publicized in 1985, those reports were never on my radar and I had been unaware of accusations by other victims. But in 2002, the national clergy abuse scandal finally broke wide open with a well-known case brought against the Boston Catholic Archdiocese. This case led to the investigation of criminal cover-ups by Catholic personnel and nine priests were criminally charged with rape and/or molestation. This also caused the resignation of their previously revered Cardinal and a settlement of $90 million to approximately 550 plaintiffs. It had, so far, been the largest individual settlement of its kind to date. Lawsuits were being filed in many dioceses around the country and several of those dioceses have since filed bankruptcy.

I'd like to think that the church had no idea what was about to blow, but I truly do believe they were preparing for this. They had, for many years, covered up their criminal acts by writing fat checks to families and sending their priests to the spa.

I hadn't really thought about it too much since I faced Stringer, except of course when it snuck in through the intimacy doors. These reports caught my attention, because up until now, I pretty much thought I was the only one; I had been isolated from any others who might have experienced this type of abuse. But the media attention slowly grew and it seemed there were hundreds, perhaps thousands of people who had experienced sexual abuse from the Catholic clergy! This was all new information for me and I was relieved and disgusted, happy that I was not alone but sad that I was not alone.

Here's what else happened in 2002: The California state Legislature passed a law suspending the statute of limitations for one full year beginning January 1, 2003, opening the door for victims to file molestation claims. Hundreds of abuse lawsuits that had been previously rejected because their allegations were too old were now invited to come forth. The California Supreme Court has a history with clergy sexual abuse cases dating back to the early 1980's; some of these cases did not end well for the victims. I was so intrigued by this that I decided to call the Archdiocese once again and see what they knew. To my surprise, they had established a Sexual Abuse Hotline. I shake my head in sorrow at how they chose to deal with this centuries old issue; how the cardinal of Los Angeles handled this gross misconduct by his staff, bringing shame on himself. The person I spoke with on the hotline took my name and number, then passed it onto a vicar of the clergy who then passed the report off to another reverend monsignor who then passed it to one father Robert Lorenzo and that's who called me back.

Lorenzo, not yet aware of what about to explode, called me the next day and gave me information I requested, which he probably should not have done. I felt uneasy talking to him and it wasn't until a few minutes into the conversation that my memory kicked in. This Robert Lorenzo had been a friend of my family back in the 1970's for he, too, had been a seminarian at Claretville. He remembered me and had been one of the many Claretians who frequently visited our home in Thousand Oaks. I vividly recall him playing Marco Polo in the pool with us kids and several other grown men who were seminarians. It was not a pleasant memory.

During our phone call, he was reading from the "Secret Files" aka the Canon 489 files (another Google point) and told me that Stringer had been accused of sexual misconduct, requested a three-month leave of absence in June of '73 [Jemez Springs Spa & Resort] and that the church had laicized him. So, Stringer had told me the truth when I confronted him! Shortly thereafter, I received a letter from Lorenzo with the Claretian Order letterhead which reads:

"The peace and love of Our Lord Jesus be with you… Should the accuser demand or request restitution, counseling, money, or any form of valuable consideration (the demand"), the policy of the Claretians is for the accuser to make the demand of the accused, former Claretian. The Claretian Missionaries are in no way responsible for satisfying such demand. If the accused, former Claretian is, in fact, guilty of the accusation made by the accuser, the Claretians believe that the accused, former Claretian is solely responsible for satisfying such demand. This is only just and right. Therefore, with your pennission (sic) I will send [Benjamin Stringer] the demand you sent me along with your address so that he may respond to it."

Nice attempt at passing the buck, but how wrong they were. I doubt if Stringer ever got the letter from Lorenzo but as you now know, I had not heard from him until I went to Seattle. Under this one-year law beginning on January 1, 2003, plaintiffs had until Dec. 31, 2003, to file suit. The law applied to all victims of sexual abuse, not just those who alleged wrongdoing by priests. Prior to this, victims could file a case only until their 26th birthday or three years after a time they could prove that they discovered they had emotional problems linked to sexual abuse. Each state has its own laws but needless to say, these laws are not sufficient enough to effectively support the victims of this crime. This new one-year law was a paradigm shift for hundreds of victims who had been previously silenced. It was certainly a game changer for me. Church attorneys argued the law was unconstitutional because it specifically targeted the Roman Catholic Church. They also stated that priest's files sought by civil and criminal attorneys in clergy abuse cases were confidential communications protected by the First Amendment, and that providing these "secret files" (which is what Lorenzo was reading from) violated the separation of church and state, creating excess bureaucracy in church affairs. These files are now made available for public viewing on the Internet.

In September of 2002, those arguments were rejected and the church was ordered to turn over files to plaintiff's attorneys. These files included communications amongst the priests; their bishop and the vicar for clergy, and also thousands of files from the church counselors. However, psychological reports were exempted for the time being.

As January 2003 loomed closer, the Church had lawyered up. This wasn't their first rodeo.

The abuse cases in California were coordinated into three geographic groups referred to as Clergy I, Clergy II and Clergy III. These groups covered the two archdioceses in Los Angeles and San Francisco, the state's 10 dioceses and many other institutions including schools and religious orders associated with the U.S. Roman Catholic Church.

Clergy I and II - Los Angeles County Superior Court oversaw the Southern California cases. Clergy I covered 556 cases against the Archdiocese of Los Angeles and the Diocese of Orange. Clergy II covered 140 cases from the Diocese of San Diego and the Diocese of San Bernardino.

Clergy III - Alameda County Superior Court oversaw the cases in that part of Northern California covering 160 cases from the dioceses of San Francisco, Oakland, Sacramento, etc.

Throughout this legislation and suits filed in other states, the problems got worse with the church's insurance carriers resisting, and in some cases refusing to cover the legal costs. Some carriers stated that the archdiocese did not follow protocol, did not report the abuses as required by the insurance policies. Seriously, the Catholic Church had actually been purchasing insurance for many years for this specific reason. They had sexual abuse insurance. Think about this... Writing checks to families was merely a tax insurance write off.

Pursuant to JCCP 4286 settlement agreement (Google that!) those confidential files became public in 2013 and what a gift! Already, just while writing this book, I have been reading previously unpublished documents from the LA Archdiocese regarding the pederasts and there are hundreds of them - both pedophiles and documents. Stringer had told me there were other girls but I had never seen any proof and no one else had come forward with allegations against Stringer during the litigation. In fact, while writing about the Seattle trip in Chapter Four, I still had this little tiny inkling of doubt as to whether or not there really were any other young girls whom he had abused.

So I took a break to look on the Internet at some of these newly released "secret files" and found a document regarding Benjamin

Stringer. Part of this file contained a copy of a hand-written letter to the same people I had contacted in the LA, several pages long, from another female who was also sexually abused in 1967 at age ten by the same priest who violated me in Southern California! The letter was dated 1993, five years after I had confronted him in Seattle!

I could barely believe what I was reading or the timing therein. It was as if she was reaching out to me through the Web. This hand-written letter was on the same screen on which I was typing; some of her words exactly mirrored my own experience. I could feel her pain as I read her letter, describing the scene and the emotional scars left within, her childhood was ripped apart. As anyone who has experienced abuse knows, especially isolating abuse such as this, validation is a huge piece in the lifelong healing which spirals around again and again throughout our lifetime! I'll never know why that woman didn't make it to the court cases, and because our names have been redacted from the documents, I may never know who she was. I hope this book someday finds its way to her hands and heart.

There were several other documents I found that day, which I have saved in my files as a type of validating trophy case. One especially caught my eye, dated March 27, 2002. In it, were letters between the clergy, monsignor and Lorenzo regarding the phone calls that I had made to the Clergy Abuse Hotline and the conversation that I had with Lorenzo during that time! I was stunned. Here I am writing this book, struggling with my own testimonial and then I find these "secret files" that had just been published for all to witness. What a relief and once again, a giant piece of validation for me.

In January 2003, it was all over the headlines. Hundreds of people were actually suing the Catholic Church in both civil and criminal court. These were not class-action suits but individuals accusing the church, the orders and the priests themselves of criminal conduct. For several months, it looked as though all of the pederasts charged were going to serve jail time. However, in June of 2003 the U.S. Supreme Court overturned the criminal aspect of that law and as a result, the charges were dropped and criminal convictions were overturned for approximately 800 California molestation suspects, including Catholic priests. Many of these men had been sent to prison, only to be released several months later and yes, they're still out there, roaming free among the masses.

Both of my parents were still living in Southern California where all the action was taking place, so I called my mom and talked about it. I don't actually know why I did this; she was not capable of helping me with this when I was a child, nor did she remember much when I asked her about it years ago. But one could only hope, so I asked if any of her attorney friends could assist me with getting some information, see how much it would cost to file a complaint. I was thinking in dollars at the time, not in emotional fare.

Mom referred me to an attorney friend of hers who basically laughed and said, "Yeah, that's not gonna go anywhere. You can't expect to sue the Catholic Church and actually win!" I can only imagine that he still regrets that conversation. And even though my dad and I had reconciled our relationship somewhat, I didn't dare ask him for a referral, it was clear that I could no longer depend on him for anything important. After seeking referrals through friends and getting nowhere, I shrugged off the idea of joining the fray. I had made my peace with Stringer and thought that was the end of this story.

And that is why I like the saying, "Don't believe everything you think." My father is living proof that with a true desire to change, anyone can turn it around, make amends, pay it forward and that's exactly what transpired. Sometime in his 50's, dad went back to school and graduated in 1996 with his Ph.D. in Clinical Psychology. He has been well trained in treating PTSD, severe sexual trauma, sexual addiction and sexual offending behavior. Because of his training and excellent reputation, he was chosen to conduct psychological evaluations of clergy abuse victims for an attorney in Costa Mesa, California named Joe Stanley. It was Stanley who dug the foxhole, hunkered down and led the troops for the long, five-year battle against the church. It was my dad who called to tell me about an attorney that I might want to contact.

Chapter Nine

My mother. People have asked me, "Where was your mother in all this?" Good question and I don't have the answer. She was working full time, dealing with an abusive husband and I truly believe she was doing her best with the tools she had. Yesterday I awoke from a dream about my mother. As with so many dreams, the environment changed every few "moments" of the dream, I have no idea if I'm talking about minutes or milliseconds but the surroundings kept me busy. The dream begins: I need to get to my mom's house, something is calling me to go see her, something is wrong and she needs help. Scene two, I enter her home as she walks by, very busy, acknowledging my presence while on the phone to someone important. Clearly she does not have time to chat with me. The surroundings continued to morph and scene three lands us in her bedroom. No longer busy, she's propped up on many pillows, seemingly ill and knowing her time is coming to an end. There are many other people in the room who are unfamiliar to me and I sit by her side, trying to provide comfort. There's a clear and present unsafe feeling, but I keep the fear at bay while she tells me it's time to go, she's going home and I cycle through the layers of grief and relief. That's the dream I have about my mother as I'm writing this chapter.

The sadness stayed with me as I opened my eyes, as if it was real and I think it kind of is. I called her that evening, as I promised myself I would and the conversation was… well, not a conversation, as usual. Calling my mother is like dialing into a pre-recorded webinar that's already in progress. It's always been this way except for about two months last year during the holiday season. Mom was doing volunteer work, filling baskets of food and clothing and helping to deliver to those in need. During that time, my mother initiated a few calls to me, asking about my life. This was highly unusual behavior for my mom and just as I began to get used to it, the calls stopped and we were back to our old routine. So the timing for the call was perfect as it had been about two weeks since my last call to my mother and it went something like this:

Mom: Hello who's this?
(Loud background noises sounded like she was at a busy cafe, but it's just the television this time)

Hiya Mom, it's me, C.M.. How ya doin'? I miss you.

Oh hey hi. Hold on. Susie, Susie it's my daughter from Minnesota calling, let me call you back. Bye. Yeah. Bye. Hiya honey hi how are you oh I'm in crisis mode serious crisis mode ya know the purchase just wasn't a good idea I made a mistake I feel awful but I thought it would be good but ya know I buy and buy out of love ya know I just need to get better control of the money situation and I should have known better but my sponsor helped me get into debtor's anonymous and so now I'm just using cash only and cut up all my credit cards and paying only the minimum payment on them all because I just can't afford it and it's just I was trying to help Carl but now he's trying to pay rent and then the truck so I'm down to my last thousand and I just need to…

Picture my head spinning around on my neck. As usual, I tried to interrupt, interject, interlocute and have a conversation but to no avail. My mother has always been this way. I did not know what purchase she was referring to until she took a breath and I was able to I quickly jump in with, "What purchase?" and she said, "What??"

So my mother spoke ad nauseum about her financial woes, once again. This is not the first time she's had to cut up all of her credit cards. Her illness, compulsive spending and an obsession with OPM (other people's money) is laminated with a beautifully clear coat of kindness and incredible social skill. People love my mother, and so do I. She has a great sense of humor, is a good storyteller, has a sharp eye for design and can speak several languages fluently. Her now-deceased husband used to tell me, "Boy, your mother knows how to work a room."

This woman, who for many years lived in a gated community on a man-made island in Southern California, could never seem to find true happiness inside her own soul. She was always concerned about what everyone else thought about her and there was never, ever enough _____. You name it: never enough money, things, decorations, people, spiritual satisfaction, attention, etc. Her $1.5 million dollar island home was filled with furniture, trinkets and expensive, flashy items from all over the world. Every horizontal surface was jammed-packed with stuff and framed photographs.

Wall space was prime real estate, too; every vertical surface was covered with paintings, multi media art, framed articles and wall hangings touting awesome, life-affirming concepts. Her home was filled with photos of her husband and herself in countless poses and outfits with many important people. I have never before or since been in a home that held so many pictures of the occupants therein. It was like an museum dedicated to the current residents.

Her garage was filled with tons more odds and ends that couldn't fit into the house. My mother had a need to fill up all the space outside of her human self so that she could avoid the emptiness and guilt that stood still within. I'll never forget the time when I witnessed her crying in the middle of her $1.5 million dollar home, surrounded with 1.5 million things, sobbing, "I have nothing to show for my life." Repugnance trickled down the back of my throat and settled into my gut.

Throughout her whole adulthood, debt was her BFF, followed by an insatiable need for approval from others. However, logic was her arch nemesis when any of her daughters tried to approach her about these issues. Mom didn't think she had a issue, really. Occasional glimpses into reality prompted yet another phase of credit creativity, but always left her standing ever closer to her own impending fiscal cliff. Several times in the last ten years, my older sister would sit down with mom, paper and pencil to show her the financial crises in which she was drowning. Mom's response was always the same, "Coffee, anyone? How about some sausage and peppers?"

I believe that it was this aversion to reality, this fantasy with how life *should* be, that caused a breach in the safety of her children. We were clothed and fed, our diapers had been changed and the house was heated but there was always her need to seek out others for attention. Her family alone was never enough; she was always inviting others into our home - church people, couples, families, many men who were priests and seminarians, some of whom were attracted to her children. I had been sexually fondled, touched, grabbed and manipulated by some of these people and both she and my father remained either unawares or in denial.

A clergyman, a friend of my parents, was sexually abusing me in their own bedroom while they were downstairs entertaining and neither of my parents had a clue.

How does that happen? How does a parent continue to ignore the fact that her so-called friends are violating her children? How can a parent be so oblivious to the changes displayed by a child who has been sexually contaminated? Adding insolence to ignorance, neither could figure it out with me many years later. "Call McClaren" she said. "Do your third step" he said. "To hell with you both" I wanted to scream.

So the answer to "Where were your parents" continues to elude me, but they obviously weren't paying attention.

Chapter Ten

In the matter of C.M. Morgan v. Los Angeles Catholic Archdiocese

Early in 2003, my father called me. This was a little out of the ordinary but welcomed. He called to tell me that he had been conducting psych evaluations for an attorney named Joe Stanley who was representing several victims of clergy sexual abuse in Los Angeles County. Dad gave me Stanley's phone number in case I was interested in looking further into this issue. How's that for making amends on a gigantic level? Throughout his psychology education, dad had to go through individual and group counseling - he had to take some good, long looks at his past behavior and actions. Between that, sobriety and who knows what else, he learned some giant life-lessons and I, like he, could not be more grateful.

So the messenger was my father! This same person, who, 15 years prior told me to "just let it go" was now connecting me to some one who would help me hold on. I had to think on it for a few days. Was I done? Did I want more? Was there another path I had heretofore unimagined? And I realized that, although I had made my peace with Stringer as an individual, there was more to see behind the scenes. Not unlike the great and powerful Oz, standing there behind the curtain, frantically pulling levers and flipping switches. I wanted to see what the church knew, what they were hiding. How many of us were sexually abused? Was it mostly boys? That's what we always hear, that pedophiles are only interested in males - which is why I believe that many people confuse pedophilia with homosexuality. So was I an anomaly? Were there other girls? Who knew what, when did they know it and what did they do about it? I wanted them to know what I knew and visa versa. I wanted the organization to hear from me, just as Stringer did 15 years earlier. And so I called the phone number given to me by my dad.

Joe Stanley - The only male whom I could truly call my hero. He is super smart, soft spoken and empathetic. He is also a powerful and highly respected attorney based in California. He has been called a Super Lawyer, has been selected as one of California's Top 100 Attorneys and has represented victims throughout the country. I'm pretty sure that he is a hero to many.

His career as a real estate attorney took an unexpected turn some years back when a friend from childhood, a former classmate at their catholic school asked Stanley for assistance in filing suit against the church. Apparently, this former classmate had been sexually abused at their school all those years ago. Stanley accepted the challenge and was one of the first attorneys to litigate and win a lawsuit against the church. That client later became an attorney, joined Stanley's firm and I'll never forget meeting him; he was the first person I ever met who had also experienced clergy abuse. It was cathartic - as we met in the big conference room for our first discussion and we shook hands, we locked eyes. We knew something together. We shared that experience of sexual abuse by catholic priests; a crappy connection but a connection nonetheless. No doubt, the details were different, but the fall out from this type of abuse is something I would not wish on anyone. And here he was, a comrade, a confidante, and another person who really understood this from the inside out. I knew I was in the right place.

Also on the team was a former attorney for the church who, after one year, was disgusted with what he saw and jumped ship. This guy brought with him a plethora of information and documentation that had not before been seen by any other lay attorneys. There were several other magnificent, intelligent, compassionate attorneys on board by the time 2003 rolled around and their team was ready to rumble. They truly were experienced, aggressive and successful.

So I had called the main number, told them my dad had referred me, was transferred to Joe's office and we spoke for about an hour. He was so kind and gentle; I was surprised by his genuine, soft-spoken manner. At the end of our first conversation, he transferred me back to his assistant who then made arrangements to fly me to Los Angeles two weeks later. The plan was that I would stay in LA for three days, meet with Joe and his team, and participate in a two-day psychiatric evaluation. The attorney's office paid for everything - the flight, accommodations, food and a rental car. The validation now was beyond anything I could have imagined. Up until this time, the only ones who truly supported and validated me were Maggie and the perpetrator himself!

While in LA, I stayed in a small hotel suite just a few blocks from the Santa Monica Pier. The pier and surrounding area is a very fun place to walk around, play, think, feel and be. The smell of the ocean waves; the sounds of the artists, ride-hawkers and a rickety roller-coaster; the perfect weather; the abundance of other humans with who knows what in their own private history books... all these things drew me to hang out on the beach and the pier whenever I was not engaged in the mission at hand.

Those three days... it's hard to write about that time because it was so surreal. Like reading a book about someone else's life. Throughout the short, one-hour flight, I felt alone but together. I was calm, not yet anxious and not yet knowing what was about to unravel. I got into my rental car, re-read the directions for the 18th time and headed to the attorney's office for my first meeting.

The office was housed in a very large, beautiful, 11-story building. After parking the car, I took my backpack, which held my important papers for this... I don't know what... litigation? Lawsuit? All I really had was the letter from the Claretian's Provincial Office in Los Angeles which basically stated that they know nothing, it's not their fault and they can't do anything about it, anyway. That paper and my story was all I brought with me. That and my younger sister who was very supportive but in hindsight, having her there that was not the best decision. I was later to learn that she had not known the whole story until that day and she was affected by it for some time.

We were greeted in a most friendly and professional manner and then escorted to Mr. Stanley's office. That was my first time seeing him and he looked exactly how I pictured him after our phone call; slightly larger build, clean-shaven and a really neat smile. I liked and trusted him right away.

Two other people entered the room - an attorney and an assistant - and we began to talk but this time, it felt for real. Joe asked me some of the same general questions from our first phone call. They listened, took notes, asked questions and more questions. They kindly asked for details, dates, places, and names. They asked if I needed anything to drink, if I needed a break, if I needed more time, or more tissues. It was hard telling them my story with all the details and how the pureness of my child self had been ruined. I had to stop and think deep about time lines and places; we were talking about events that had occurred almost 40 years prior. Then I told them how I confronted Stringer in Seattle when I was 28 years old and how he admitted his part, made amends and paid for half my airline ticket. They sat in silence and in awe that I had tracked him down and challenged his reality. I had to do it, though. Sexual perpetrators are able to continue their vulgar behavior because the victims are often silenced. I would not be quiet about this; my story is one of thousands similar and they should all be told. There are still plenty of "believers" who do not believe us.

After meeting with them for a few hours, I headed to the hotel suite where I met my mom and sisters. I could have stayed with any of them as they all lived within an hour of the hotel, but it felt best to have my own place to be alone and quiet. We ordered pizza and salad and I talked with them about what the next few days and years may entail. My older sister was shocked, she had no idea any of this had occurred. I had not known that. Isn't it odd how something so severe can occur inside a home and your own siblings are unawares? This is the awesome skill and intent of perpetrators; to keep the secrets and carry on as normal.

My mother cried. She seemed incredulous, even though we had visited this topic several years back. Even though she had, in her mind, taken care of it way back then. Tears of guilt flowed freely down her cheeks.

As usual, my mother began to speak much about her experience of the whole matter, her sorrow, her guilt, her anger and her self. She wasn't without compassion and support, but it was blended with a full dose of what it was like for her. This behavior was tolerable but annoying. My second oldest sister brought some light to the issue and this took me by surprise. I didn't know what she knew but according to her, I confided in her about Stringer shortly after one of the molestations had occurred. She said that I had told her what happened, then she told my parents, then they told someone else who told Stringer to leave the church. That sounds nice and clean but unfortunately, no one else could corroborate this version and although we had to leave it as her memory, it was still another level of validation. Someone knew something at the time, but no one ever told me.

After my sisters and mom left the hotel, I was alone for the evening with all the unknowns ahead and memories past fresh from telling story. The next day I drove to a psychologist's office somewhere in Los Angeles. Oh the freeways are so complicated, winding all over LA, they provided an odd comfort in not knowing where I was headed. The woman who saw me was perfect for her job, put me right at ease and I immediately trusted her as well. She spoke to me soft and caring, kind and empathetic. Again, I had to tell the story, answer many questions and give many details. There were paper tests, followed by more dialogue with the doctor. It was a little easier telling it this time, still in my heart from the day before as more memory seeped in and escaped onto her notes. After an exhausting six hours, I headed back to the hotel, had dinner and took an evening walk on the pier. It felt good to be alone and not talk anymore. It felt good to be believed.

At the end of the pier stood a large Ferris wheel with the old type of open-air bench seats. It was awesome, standing 90 feet above the pier and a full 130 feet above the ocean! I envied the courageous ones enjoying the ride. It looked so freeing and gentle; I imagined that it felt disconnected and almost wild in its slowness. I had never been on a Ferris wheel; I could not get over my fear. Heights scared me, took my belly for a spin. So I just watched and imagined, settled into my grounded comfort but wishing that I, too, could fly over the waves below. The sun set below the horizon as only a Southern California sunset can and I felt at peace.

The next morning I was back at the psychologist's office for some more conversation and the test results were in that showed I was, in fact, telling the truth, the whole truth and nothing but the truth. Although going over the story so many times was emotionally trying, I caught myself wincing often enough, I was very comfortable with all of this testing. It was clear that the attorneys needed to be sure they had a true, solid case with which to move forward. After all, one must have a logical, methodical approach when bringing litigation against the great and powerful church.

That afternoon, I headed back at the attorney's office again, for some final decisions. "Yes" I answered, "I want to move forward," another life-changing sentence. Stanley asked me what type of financial compensation I might be looking for and I told him I would like a few thousand for all the therapy and the other half of my airline ticket from 20 years ago when I confronted Stringer. He laughed gently, not at me, but at the meekness of my humility and then said something like, "Oh, you'll get that, but we're going for seven figures, sweetie, not four." He wasn't kidding. The meeting ended, I hugged my attorney whom I barely knew and then I headed back to the hotel. When I write about it, I can still feel that hug in my bones… it was so comforting.

Again, I had dinner alone and walked the pier, content with my inner solitude. Thinking on the past two days, the conversations, the validations, the tears, the tests, the incredulity of what was unfolding, I began to feel this slow, huge surge in my heart and this amazing freedom flowing throughout my body. I, C.M. Morgan, was suing the Roman Catholic Archdiocese of Los Angeles

County, The Claretian Missionaries of Los Angeles County and Benjamin Stringer of Seattle, Washington. I mean... like, who does that?? Well, apparently I do. I was so proud of myself; I had, once again and with much support, done the unthinkable! By the time I got to the end of the pier, I felt emotionally and mentally uplifted. I was high, filled with gratitude and a sense of fearlessness, and then I noticed where I was standing. Looking straight up above me stood the big, giant Ferris wheel. I stared for a few minutes, took a deep breath and bought a ticket for one.

It creaked, groaned and started slowly backward, then up, stopping every few feet to let others off and on. I held my breath in complete exhilaration, slowly exhaling as needed. Rolling slowly to the top, we stopped, of course, but surprisingly, I was not scared. My bench-seat swayed over the ocean, my heart pounded, tiny tears welled up in my eyes but I truly was not scared. I was doing it. I felt brave again, amazingly free and full of light at the top of that Ferris wheel on Santa Monica Pier.

Chapter Eleven

The next five years were filled with litigious motion after motion as the church continued to cover-up allegations, dodge the questions, hire more lawyers and fight the wrong fight. Their actions were abhorrent and as such, the courts ordered them, time and again, to reveal their most secret files. There were thousands upon thousands of pages dating back many years.

Emotionally, I could not keep current with the litigation; it was too much for me. Things changed weekly, sometimes daily and my dream-team attorneys stayed on top of every detail. As the church continued to bring more litigators through the revolving doors, I would, on occasion, receive yet another interrogatory with yet another set of inquiries but in slightly different formats. It was gross, really, the way these Catholics denied the very tenets for which they say they believe. But as the old saying goes, you can't save your ass and your face at the same time, so they endured for five long years, trying to save face. I truly believe that they knew they could not save their archaic arses. It was just a matter of time as they tried but failed to show that it wasn't as bad as it seemed. Shortly before their cardinal was to take the stand, the church settled. They did not admit anything, of course, but they agreed to disagree. The attorneys had settled upon a rubric for how victims would get compensated depending on the severity and longevity of abuse. I cannot imagine being on that committee, but I'm grateful that someone was.

All of this information and everything you ever wanted to know about how these cases were processed can now be found on the Internet. The church was court-ordered to make those documents public during the middle of 2013.

My lawsuit began in 2003 and in 2004 I met Kari, with whom I fell in love and married in San Francisco in 2005 - thank you Mayor. The marriages were not legal, however, and we were asked to mail our marriage certificate back to the state so they could refund $45.00 for the marriage license. We didn't do that, but we did separate a few years later, just after the settlement. As this lawsuit was based on unwanted sexual contact, oddly enough it bookended my relationship with Kari who, for reasons I'll never understand, withheld the intimacy I so craved. It was slight insanity for me. Kari would flirt with me and be physical when we were around our friends but as soon as we got home, hers was a no-contact zone. It was subtle, at first, and then when it became obvious I tried talking with her to no avail. She denied that there was an issue at all. She had lost interest within one year of our relationship but wanted to stay together as a mostly platonic couple.

Lynn pleaded, "Look, my friend Sara doesn't like sex either. Can't we just cuddle?" and on it went. Several days before the wedding, she told me that she could live her whole life without any sexual contact. This floored me, I remember standing in the living room, looking at her and the rest of my life. Thinking of how much planning and money we had spent on the wedding. I saw a split in the road ahead and chose to stay the course, hoping she might change. She didn't.

Throughout this legal action, which was centered on unwanted sexual abuse, I was in a relationship with a woman who did not want any sexual contact at all. I know, go figure. Kari also wasn't the type to dive into feelings and process what ever is going on under the skin. When the interrogatories came in the mail, or when I had conversations with my attorney, I would bend into a melancholy mood for a day or two. Kari never understood this and would ask, "What is the problem? It happened so long ago, there's nothing you can do about it now." She also racked up thousands of dollars of mutual debt, but that's another story.

By May of 2007 I was empty, tired, lonely and slinking into an unforeseen depression. Kari had left for the summer to work at her full time job that moved to the Midwest for the summer months. I was unable to deal with much by then, my head and heart were a mess and I began drinking daily, barely making it to work. Playing around on the Internet I found a good listener, which led to a short, unfulfilling affair.

Then in July of 2007, the phone call came. That summer, I, too was working part time in the same Midwest office as Kari. In between our duties and my studying at the local library, she and I tried to repair something that was permanently broken. I was also finishing up my on-line courses at the University of Northern Colorado, having been enrolled in a yearlong Legal Interpreter Training Program. Under the Registry of Interpreters for the Deaf (RID), a national organization and certifying body for Sign Language Interpreters, I had already received my Certificate of Interpretation and Certificate of Transliteration many years back. Now I was working toward the often coveted and sometimes feared SC:L - the Specialist Certificate: Legal.

One afternoon while at the summer office, a colleague called out, "C.M.! Phone call for you!" How Joe Stanley found me there I'll never know. Surrounded by my inner chaos with Kari, his voice on the other end was welcoming and soft.

> "Hiya sweetheart. It's me Joe. How ya doin'? Are you sitting down?"

> "Wow, hi Joe. No I'm standing up. Is everything okay?"

> "Everything is good, but you should sit down for this one."

So once again I did what he told me to do. Then he said that the lawsuit had been settled earlier that morning. He told me some of the details and all of the settlement agreements. He wanted my approval to sign the papers.

My mouth went dry, my heart was pounding, my body was shaking, tears welled up in my eyes and I approved.

> "We won, sweetie. We won. You did the right thing, you stayed strong and true and I am so proud of you. Congratulations..."

Can you believe it? I sued the Los Angeles Catholic Archdiocese, the Claretian Order of Seminarians and Benjamin Stringer and I won. I won! I felt a million different feelings, thought a million other thoughts but especially this: Fuck them, I won.

I was relieved to not be alone when the call came in. All the gals in the office knew of the lawsuit, so when I shared my news, I was surrounded with love and comfort. A few weeks later, I flew back home to Oakland and for the rest of that year I was kind of numb. My attorneys could have wired the check, but I chose to fly to LA and see them in person. I wanted to thank them for all their work, due diligence and their amazing kindness amidst all that crap they dealt with on a daily basis for the past five years.

After sending each of my sisters a check, just because I wanted them to have some of the church's change, I wrote another one to an organization in Oakland, CA called "Deaf Hope" whose mission is to end domestic and sexual violence through empowerment, education and services. Then I paid off over 50k worth of debt accrued by Kari and myself. An oversight on my part, I had not been aware of how much debt we had created during our short time together. Eventually I quit my job, lost contact with friends and continued to drink. I felt very lost and extremely alone. My one good pal, June, who lived in an apartment behind our home, was my steady connection to reality. She talked with me, helped me to stay light, encouraged me to keep hold of my heart and follow the path that was rolled out before me. I'm forever grateful to her for her kind words of wisdom.

I also met a woman on-line who lived in Melbourne, Australia and in January of 2008 I flew to the Big Island of Hawai'i for a few days to visit a friend and take in the natural beauty of that lush Aloha. Then I flew to Sydney, Australia and met my on-line pal. The next six months were such a fresh time for me, I felt like I could finally exhale. We toured around in Sydney for a week or so then went back to her home in Melbourne. A week later, my mother asked to borrow $5,000.00. "… just for a month or two" she said. Loaning my mother five grand would be like loaning an alcoholic a bottle of Gin; you know you'll never see that again! I suggested that maybe she try to sell one of the three cars in the garage, or the baby grand piano in the living room, or any number of pricey items in her gated community island home. I was disgusted and disheartened by her desire to get her hands on some of the settlement. That money had been given to me partly because of her neglect. It was partly because my parent's lack of focus that I was sexually abused; this was not a secret. I had to forgive her, though, because she could not see past herself and she had no idea how her behavior affected me. As I stated earlier, my mom suffered from OPM and mine was no exception.

Melbourne house was home base for the next six months. While in Australia, I found my way back to myself, once again, to that core that was suffocated so long ago. Even though meeting and forgiving Stringer healed a very crucial layer, the five year lawsuit and the relationship to Kari took me to a deeper level of sorrow and introspect that needed attention.

Australia could not have been a more perfect place for me to go and the Aussie people were consistently wonderful and welcoming! Adventure called and I traveled throughout the country visiting pals in Sydney, Adelaide, Perth and Brisbane; Explored the pre-historic island of Tasmania; Went SCUBA diving 17 times on the Great Barrier Reef, the Whitsunday Islands, Heron and Rottnest Islands; Went Hang gliding twice over the ocean in Cape Byron; Enjoyed a five-mile Skyrail tram over the rainforest from Barron Falls to Kuranda; Took helicopter rides over the Gold Coast & a bi-plane tour over Fraser Island; Toured the Koala Hospital and rescue foundation in Port Maquarie, New South Whales; Spent time at the Australia Zoo in Beerwah, Queensland, celebrating the infamous Crocodile Hunter; I swam, ran or hiked everyday; Saw amazing wildlife everywhere, especially in the people at the open air Aussie markets; Found adventure at every turn and after one month, found myself back in the rooms of Alcoholics Anonymous. I stayed physically & spiritually sober through it all thanks to the welcoming members of AA Australia.

In April, I flew to Adelaide for a second time and rented a campervan. When we finished the paperwork at the counter, the employee escorted me to the parking lot. We did a walk around as he pointed out some key features and then left me to it. It was a sweet little camper complete with stove, fridge, freezer, sink & microwave oven. In Australia, the driver's side is on the right and we also drive on the right side of the road. I had become accustomed to driving rental cars the past four months but they all had automatic transmissions. This campervan was a stick shift and although the accelerator was under my right foot, the gear shifter was on my left as was the radio, emergency brake, and passenger seat. I had to laugh at myself jolting back and forth in that parking lot for a half hour until I got a feel for it, then off I went… albeit not very smoothly.

That last two-month solo journey was unplanned and perfect. I first drove to home base in Melbourne to pack what I needed for the long trip. In honor of my rebirth, I shaved my head clean - a most liberating and beautifying event. I loved being bald and then keeping it coiffed with a #1 buzz cut, which is about ¼ inch of fuzz. During this time of sightseeing and travel, my insides were shifting as I became once again familiar with my spiritual core. I drove all the way up the east coast, spending much time alone, in quiet meditation above and below the ocean's surface. I camped at out-of-the-way places, off the beaten path or sometimes at places with facilities so I could wash my clothes. Occasionally finding solitude as the only camper in any given place, my favorite was a site near Byron Bay called, ironically, Broken Head. I stayed there for two weeks, seeing practically no one except when I was taking surfing lessons, scuba diving or walking around the nearby town. Since then, the Arakwal people have reclaimed it in 2009 as Broken Head Holiday Park. But when I was there, it was just a few camping spots, a small structure with restrooms and miles of uninhabited Oceanside beauty… perfect for healing my own little broken head.

The journey took me to amazing places both geographically and psychologically. I even got to visit Janice, a new friend on the Sunshine Coast that I had met while I was diving off Heron Island three months earlier. Janice was the girl-with-guitar island entertainment and we still stay in contact. She just cut her first album and has been an inspiration for me to finish this book. My journey in Australia was documented via a series of short stories which I published on a website throughout the six months.

Chapter Twelve

I want to back up in my story a bit, before I left for Australia…

There had been a six-month stretch of time between the phone call from Stanley and my journey to Oz. I left the Midwest without a sense of where I was headed and my relationship with Kari was already feeling in the past tense, even though we went to therapy twice before my trip down under to see if there was any oil left in the engine. For those mechanically inclined, it was as though I was calibrating my internal combustion chambers with a Go/No-Go feeler gauge; this spot is too loose, undecided, too much slack, detached. A nanosecond further is too tight, too much pressure, immoveable and rigid. Still living at the house I shared with Kari, I didn't know whether to stay or go. She continued on with her summer job and seemingly out of nowhere, I was called to interpret out in the middle of the ocean. Surrounded by water, on a ship with people I didn't know and an opportunity to travel someplace new. Perfect timing, I jumped on board!

Fate reared its lovely head and I found myself working on a huge cruise ship with over 100 other interpreters and several thousand deaf guests. It was somewhere between the islands of Dominica and Martinique that I met my future and current bride, Ashlynn. We never were assigned to work together but somehow, amongst these thousands of people, we briefly connected at the pool and in the bar.

I honed my interpreting craft and profession in the San Francisco Bay Area. By the time I accepted the assignment at sea, I had been ensconced in the field for 15 years. The Bay Area is known in these circles for spawning some of the most incredibly skilled Sign Language Interpreters and as such, I knew several of the interpreters who were also on that ship. Most of the other interpreters were from all over the country, including Ashlynn, and I made acquaintances fast. It's easy for me to connect to complete strangers, but I did not get close to anyone. No one would know the anguish I was feeling at the time. I never showed it, never talked to any of my colleagues about the massive life-changing events I was going through. I had stayed positive and happy on the outside hoping my inside would someday catch up. As well, I spent as much time alone as possible, which wasn't much time at all. I remember chatting with Ashlynn, but nothing stood out for me with her or anyone. I was struggling to keep my hands above water.

Ashlynn was only six years into the interpreting field and from a small town in Minnesota. Her experience onboard was first filled with fear of the unknown, and then filled with observation and fascination. She remembers me well; I was one of her fascinations.

We had a vastly different experience on the same exact itinerary, I do not remember her very well at all. In rehashing the story years later, she recounts, "I thought you were so cool and connected, hanging out with the cool kids and just being free and easy. People were drawn to you!" She also thought I had hooked up with one of the other interpreters, which was not true as it was the furthest thing from my mind. I danced with lots of women, an excellent outlet when feeling the funk, and I joked and laughed but still, it was a very rough time in my life. To Kari's dismay, I chose to work on several more cruises during the time she was in the Midwest and also after she came home. I no longer trusted her nor believed in her or us, so I needed to get away and the cruise assignments were a perfect solution. One day, while in therapy, I tried to talk about the concept of feeling so undesired by my partner bookended by the litigation of unwanted sexual perversion. The therapist agreed with Kari, stated that it was so long ago and should not be a factor in our relationship. I may not be an expert in psychology, but I knew the two concepts were spiraled around each other and I needed to go away and heal. The deep blue Caribbean blessed my grief and each cruise had steered me closer to the decision to leave.

I digress, back to Australia... Six months into my Aussie adventures, it was time to go back to the states. Even though I had a 12-month tourist visa and several employment opportunities there, something was pulling me back home. I stayed with my mom in Southern California from June to December, and then found a small in-law unit to rent back up in Oakland. The owner lived in the big house up front. She was a wonderful landlord, another Lesbian friend, easy to chat with and a psychotherapist by trade. I felt blessed to be living so close to her.

My beloved and faithful dog of 13 years, Ricki Marie, had been staying with my mom and developed cancer while I was gone. Although his symptoms didn't appear until we moved back to Oakland, it was obvious by then that he only had a few months to live. I was glad to have come home. We were together just about 24/7 during his last few weeks as I wasn't working much then. It was good for us in that little, 850 square foot home and when his time came, the nurse arrived with the special sleeping medicine.

My friends Annie, June and her doggie/Ricki's best friend Bodhi joined us. It was the most beautiful passing and I cried as he went so easy and peacefully. This happened right before I left for another passage through the Caribbean Seas, an assignment that held only about 75 deaf guests and only five other interpreters. Ashlynn happened to be one of those five.

There are approximately 12,000 Sign Language Interpreters registered with the RID and hundreds, perhaps thousands of others who are not members nor are they certified. You may not know this, but at any given time, cruise ships the world over are traveling with any number of deaf guests and Sign Language Interpreters. Any ship touching American soil or territories thereof, is required to follow the Americans with Disabilities Act.

Out of all those interpreters and all those ships and all those itineraries, both Ashlynn & I were two of the six on this particular assignment. I had met her briefly in 2007 and here we were eating at the same table two years later in the middle of the world. We could not have been any more different from each other.

Me: A 48 year old Dyke, "out" since I was 16, schooled in all things Lesbian and liberal, I had been raised by Amazons and Crones at Womyn's Music Festivals, The Brick Hut Café, Marin Vehicle Repair and countless other coffee houses, book stores, bars and venues created by women for women in general and Lesbians in particular. I was sober, had few friends in my life, single and sworn to never get involved with another woman, especially a straight one.

She: A 28-year-old housewife, schooled in all things small town and heterosexual. She had been raised by the best parents a kid could ask for and despite her mom wanting her to stay home and have babies, Ashlynn was crazy about travelling. She had been a master leader, taking women and individuals with disabilities on trips throughout the Boundary Waters Canoe Area. She led high school girls on two 30-day canoe trips into Northern Canadian routes; Was a crew member of four women on a 40-day canoe trip from Northern Canada leading into the Hudson Bay; Had been a soccer coach for both girls and boys varsity team as well as a team of youth with cognitive impairments. As well, she was a party woman, had lots of friends she had grown up with and was the center of her social circle.

During the weeklong assignment on this cruise, our team leader never had us working together. It was an oversight on her part, nothing purposefully done but odd for such a small group. The six of us crewed-up at the dinner table each evening to share fun stories from the day's excursions and discuss the next day's agenda. We also planned a roving theme party for one of the nights. It began in Emily & Jenna's cabin, they were from Florida but they didn't decorate much so the party quickly moved to the cabin I was sharing with our dear and now deceased friend Amy. Being from California, we turned up the heater, had put sand in the tiny shower with a little tiny sand shovel & a tiny beach towel and we dressed up as pirates, kind of, after having been docked on the island of Bermuda where they sell lots of Pirate paraphernalia. When the other four interpreters knocked on the door, we answered wearing eye patches, grass skirts and pirate bras made of cruise ship coasters held together by string. We. Could. Not. Stop. Laughing. Even to this day, every time I look at the photo someone snapped as we answered the door, I truly do laugh out loud. Amy was the funniest event that ever happened to anyone and all those she touched miss her.

The last stop was at Shea and Ashlynn's cabin, the Minnesota girls! They had turned their thermostat down to freezing, scattered ice cubes on the floor, bundled up in towels made to look like winter wear and took us ice fishing right there in their little tiny cabin. Oh we had so much fun and it was the first time of many that I saw Ashlynn's amazingly creative side.

As the week moved on, she and I became intrigued with one another but never let on. One night before Ashlynn arrived to dinner, I shared an idea with the other four interpreters. "Let's tell the waiters that it's her birthday tomorrow night and have a surprise party for her right here at dinner!" They all agreed and the next night I brought a birthday card to the table that we had all signed. I had also purchased a very nice rose corsage for her and I could hear my own little voice saying over and over again, "A rose?? What're you doing? What're you doing?" I liked her, that's all.

As dessert was about to be served, our waiter gave us the wink. All of a sudden there were several waiters and lots of guests at other tables signing and signing Happy Birthday to Ashlynn! Oh man, she was such a good sport and everyone wished her well as they left the dining room.

On the last night of the cruise, we both were off duty and loosely agreed at dinner to tentatively meet up in the theater to watch our colleagues interpret that night's performance. I was very nonchalant about it but was truly excited to hopefully just hang out with her. Of course, nothing would come of this - she's 20 years my junior and I'm single and, and, and...

The performance had already begun and I walked into the theater on the second floor wearing fancy blue jeans and a purple pullover cotton shirt with a ¾ length sleeve. I never wear purple but had brought it for something different. If you ever have the opportunity to look inside the wardrobe closet of a Caucasian Sign Language Interpreter, you are apt to see nothing but black, grey and dark blue attire. Due to the nature of this visual language we interpret, we need to be easy on the eyes of the receiver so we wear clothes contrasting our skin color. Purple is acceptable in some venues, but not very appealing. Although it was not my favorite, I had not worn it all week and it was the cleanest shirt I had.

Ashlynn walked in just about the same time, on the same second floor, wearing fancy blue jeans and... a purple cotton pullover shirt. We laughed, chatted to each other in sign, blushed, watched Amy's magical skill interpret the show and I resisted the urge to fall in love.

We all disembarked the next morning, only to realize that we had a six-hour wait for our respective flights at the airport. As it happens, there is a Botanical Garden nearby so Amy, Shea, Ashlynn and I hopped on the tram and went for a tour. After some time, Amy and Shea went back to the airport and Ashlynn and I stayed on the tram, seated on opposites sides of the same bench. I wanted to sit close and she did too but neither of us moved. We then strolled through the Garden and Wildlife Park, me and nature girl. It was so refreshing to be with her. On our walk, she spotted an Eagle, which I had trouble seeing. So she leaned in close to show me from her sight level. I could smell her pure, midwestern softness as she kept her hand on the small of my back, pointing to that majestic bird. Of course, I struggled to believe that anything more would come of this friendship and right in the middle of that thought, the Eagle took flight. Seriously.

Epilogue

Summer 2013 — Pahoa, HI

After all the healing, learning, growing and loving, I still sometimes get triggered. I still cannot go into churches and have no desire to talk with anyone connected to the clergy. My stomach knots whenever I see a priest and my heart aches every time I read about another case of clergy sexual abuse. I am sickened but not surprised at how the men at the Vatican deal with this horrific abuse; It is still happening in this country and the world over.

All that said, I have learned to forgive those who have caused so much hurt on so many levels. Meeting with Bill Stringer gave me a perspective that I had never taken into consideration. I have since repaired the relationships with both my mother and father over the years and I'm grateful to have the tools to do so. My parents did the best they could with what they had; they really are pretty great folks! As well, I have forgiven myself for all the unkindness I projected inward and outward to others. We all have our own path to walk, our own challenges to face and the gifts to share from those triumphs.

When I meet a kindred soul of similar experience, I embrace our journey and the power of love. And as I sit here now, looking out at the ocean just beyond a 20-year-old lava flow in the lower Puna region of Pahoa, I feel grateful, blessed and honored. I am back in Hawai'i. My Pops and Marilyn will be arriving in a few days, he'll be officiating the wedding between Ashlynn and I. Life, this.

The End

CPSIA information can be obtained at www.ICGtesting.com
Printed in the USA
BVOW04s0824080214

344297BV00002B/3/P